the
LOTUS
TATTOO

ONE WOMAN'S GRIT
FROM BULLY TO REDEMPTION

MARISA JONES

The Lotus Tattoo: One Woman's Grit from Bully to Redemption
Published by Spirit Dog Press
Denver, CO

Names: Jones, Marisa, author.
Title: The lotus tattoo : one woman's grit from bully to redemption / by Marisa Jones.
Description: First trade paperback original edition. | Denver [Colorado] : Spirit Dog Press, 2020. | Also published as an ebook.
Identifiers: ISBN 978-0-578-56694-8
Subjects: LCSH: Child abuse. | Bullying. | Spiritual healing
BISAC: BIOGRAPHY & AUTOBIOGRAPHY / Personal Memoirs.
Classification: LCC HV5132 | DDC 362.8–dc22

Cover design by Amy Hayes
Interior design by Victoria Wolf
Author photo by Jennifer Evans

QUANTITY PURCHASES: Schools, companies, professional groups, clubs, and other organizations may qualify for special terms when ordering quantities of this title. For information, email mjones@spiritdogpress.com.

Dedicated to those who are survivors.

INTRODUCTION

I LOVE ME. Not in a pretentious or narcissistic way. I'm not a cocky person, although sometimes my ego might think otherwise. I love me as in I love myself, the woman I am today, the woman I am to become, and even the young girl I was to get here. I couldn't always say that about myself.

Years ago in a meditation workshop, I was asked to look into a mirror at myself and say the words "I love you." I didn't realize until that moment how hard that would be for me. Other women in our circle did it with ease and honesty. But I hesitated, terrified at the thought of performing this action—which was so personal—for all to see, especially when I didn't believe it.

When I finally mustered up the courage to say it, I felt like a fraud. My discomfort was so obvious that our instructor stopped what she was saying and instead talked to us about the struggles people have with those three little words. I felt vulnerable and ashamed and sorry for myself.

This small act of expressing love toward myself made me realize how broken I was. Who was I? Why didn't I feel the love for myself that others so easily could?

It would be several years before I could look into a mirror and say those three beautiful words with truth. Now, I say them daily: "I love you." "You are beautiful," I add.

Today, I am aware.

I am thoughtful.

I am grateful.

I am giving.

I am patient.

I am loving.

I am spiritual.

I am a teacher.

I am a student.

I am at peace.

I am a mother, a wife, a grandmother, a daughter, a sister, a friend, a colleague.

I am perfect, I am me, and I love me.

Before I was able to say these words, I was living in the past, a victim of my circumstances who couldn't get past the emotional pain. I was feeling completely alone and scared, questioning my mental state and concerned about my ability to raise my kids. I was empty inside. I needed help, but I didn't know where or how to find it. I just knew I had to fix me. I was going to heal myself, to see if it was possible to really be happy.

In this book, I tell you my story, starting with how I became so broken in the first place and the long journey I took to loving myself. If you're reading this, it may be because you are looking for somewhere to turn, looking for some inspiration, some hope. I offer you my story with the hope that in reading it you find yourself not alone. I am here with you. I am in your circle. And perhaps through my story, you will find the inspiration you are looking for to find your own path and make sense of your past so you can live in your present and future moments with an honest, open heart and love for yourself.

1

THE VICTIM

FROM THE TIME I WAS a small child, I have always categorized my life in chapters. Not intentionally, but in my head over the years, I compartmentalized each chapter by how I defined its ending. These chapters were kept locked up, hidden deep inside me. I knew anyone who found their contents would surely crucify me for these secrets, judging me for what was inside.

I gave each one a title: Child Abuse, Drug and Alcohol Abuse, Infertility, and Divorce. Putting a name to a chapter made sense to me, and I thought it would make sense to others. For years I lived with the shame of these chapters of my past. Naming them allowed me to define myself. The more I spoke these words, these chapter titles, the stronger I felt like I knew who I was.

As time went on, I proudly revealed my chapters to others—all neatly labeled. The contents were still locked up, but at least the chapter titles had been taken out of the closet. This allowed me to reveal myself ever so slightly without the shame of telling the stories inside. No details, no justification, no taking accountability for my actions—just four chapters, each with its own title. That was growth for me. *That's it—I'm healed*, I thought. *I can let everyone see what I am made of, and all is good, right? Just don't let anyone peek inside.*

What I didn't realize then was that with the fear and shame of my past, I had built a wall around me. I had compartmentalized my life into blocks, used those blocks to build the wall, and then sealed it with a curse. A curse I placed upon myself, the curse of a victim. While those chapters protected me from those around me and their judgment of who I was, I lived in constant fear. This self-inflicted curse led me through a life of anger, resentment, and ego, devoid of any emotions or sense of self.

I GREW UP just outside New York City to parents who had immigrated by boat from Sicily to New York in 1961 when my oldest sister, Rosetta, was just nine months old. My family was not unusual since there were a lot of immigrants in New York. My family spoke only Sicilian until my siblings and I took classes in English as a second language in primary school. We were not rich, but we always had a home, family, and food. But inside our home we held a dark secret: my dad was a violent and abusive alcoholic.

My earliest memory of my dad is when I was around three years old. My dad's birthday is the day before mine, so we always celebrated our birthdays together, along with my grandparents, aunts and uncles, cousins, and my godparents.

That day I was wearing a white-and-blue dress. I was excited for my birthday. The smell of my mom's cooking—lasagna, sautéed zucchini, and a roast in the oven—permeated the entire house. My parents had bought a cake for me with icing that read, "Happy Birthday Marisa, 3 years." Seeing that cake brought me so much happiness. In hindsight I didn't realize how much that cake would mean to me since that was the last year my name was on a cake all on its own. In later years, my cakes always read, "Happy Birthday, Frank and daughter Marisa." I grew to despise having to share my cake with someone I hated.

The party started with us kids running around enjoying playtime while the grown-ups sat at the table talking and drinking beer and whiskey. After a few hours my dad's drinking took over.

"You're stupid," he yelled at my mother when he didn't agree with one of her opinions.

My mom was hard and stubborn. She fought back. "You're the stupid one," she'd reply.

My dad's rage grew as he started his usual chant: "You called me stupid? I make the money. I feed all these fucking kids. *I'm king*—you're fucking nothing, you stupid woman!"

My mother retreated into the kitchen to do her "busy work" so she didn't have to be around him. We could all hear him yelling at her from the dining room table until one of my aunts went to my mom in the kitchen.

"Don't encourage him," my aunt told her. "Don't talk back—it only makes him angrier."

I felt bad for my mom. She was strong and a fighter, but she always had to back down to this man who called her names. It wasn't so he wouldn't attack her—my dad never hit my mom directly unless she was jumping in to protect us kids—she did it for us. The angrier my dad got, even if his anger was toward my mom, the more he took it out on us kids.

When it was time for dinner, we all returned to the table to eat. I couldn't wait to eat my mom's delicious lasagna, but midway through the meal my stomach started to ache. My stomach ached a lot when I ate. I always attributed it to the stress of being around my dad when he was drunk and angry, especially when he was yelling at my mom.

I stopped eating, and that's when my dad's rage escalated.

"Eat your dinner!" he yelled.

"My stomach hurts," I answered.

All the grown-ups tried to get me to eat. "Just eat your dinner," they said, coaxing me into eating while looking at my father in a fearful way. They knew what was coming.

"I can't eat. My stomach hurts!"

"Eat your fucking dinner!"

I started to cry. I couldn't eat—my stomach was filled with

a stabbing pain that pierced through my belly and shot up my back. The pain was unbearable. And in that moment, my dad flew into a rage.

He stood up and ripped his belt out of his pants so quickly he was like Indiana Jones and his whip. He started hitting me with the belt while I sat at the table trying to cover myself with my arms.

The other grown-ups pleaded, "Frank, stop!"

My mom jumped out of her chair to come to my rescue. I fell to the floor. My dad hovered over me, swinging his belt and hitting me all over my body. My mom frantically tried to push him off of me to stand between us. While she took some of the blows, trying to protect me, I saw my moment of escape. I ran up the stairs to my room as fast as I could. I lay in my bed crying.

"I hate you!" I yelled from my room. I could hear my dad yelling at my mom as she ran after me up the stairs. She rushed into the room and sat beside me, hugging me and trying to console me.

She held me until I stopped crying. Then she asked me, "Why didn't you eat your dinner? If you just ate, he wouldn't have gotten mad at you." As if it was my fault for antagonizing him. I loved my mom and wanted to be strong, just like her, but I was angry that she wanted me to act differently when I'd done nothing wrong.

After my tears stopped, my mother convinced me to go downstairs to have cake. I was hurting from my dad's beating, but I knew the rules. I had to go down, or my dad would come up and beat me some more until I did.

When I came downstairs everyone was waiting for me. The cake was on the table, and everyone welcomed me back. The candles were lit, and they told me to stand in front and make a wish. As I climbed up onto the chair, the grown-ups reminded me that if I had just eaten, my dad wouldn't have had to hit me. *I hate you all*, I thought to myself, and I made my wish. I wished my dad was dead.

After I blew out the candles, my dad grabbed me and pulled me onto his lap, along with my sister Gina, for a picture. Gina was a year older than I was, and she was my dad's favorite. I liked my sister, but as we grew older, I realized she thought like the others—that all I had to do was eat and not make my dad angry. I didn't want to sit on his lap. I hated him for beating me, and his breath smelled like alcohol, which made my stomach ache even more. His anger was diffused by that time, but I knew if I didn't comply, his rage would return. I climbed onto his lap and started to cry.

My dad held me closer and gave me a smile. In Sicilian he said, "*Parcesepare,*" pronounced par-chess-e-par-re. It was his nickname for me, the Sicilian word for a small, hyper, flitty bird, like a hummingbird. I always liked when he called me by that name because it was in those moments I felt that he loved me. For a brief moment I felt loved—until he added, "*Parcesepare, perché non mi ascolti?*" Little Bird, why don't you listen to me?

I have pictures of that day with me in my white-and-blue dress—one of me sitting on my dad's lap crying and one of just me and my cake. In that latter one, I look at the camera with a blank stare, mad-mugging the universe. Those pictures are very painful to look at since that is how most of my childhood played out.

As part of our strong Catholic upbringing, every night before bed my mom made us say our prayers. As we knelt beside our beds, with our hands together, my mom led us through the prayers of the "Hail Mary" and "Our Father." After our prayers, we bowed our heads in silence while my mom prayed beside us for our family, friends, food on the table, and whatever else she thought of for the day. I never paid attention to what she was saying because that was my time to talk to God, and I had a few things to say to him:

Dear God, please let my dad die in his sleep tonight—pleeeaasse. Why do I have to suffer like this? Please, God, don't let him kill me before he dies. I don't understand. Please, Jesus, if you are there, please help stop the suffering. Why am I suffering like this? Please, God. I don't want him to hurt us anymore. Please make him die in his sleep tonight. Please make him die in his sleep tonight. Please make him die in his sleep tonight. Amen.

I was four years old. My mom had no idea I was praying for my dad to die. I couldn't tell her or anyone else. It was wrong to pray for someone to die. I knew that, and I was afraid to let my mom know I was praying something so evil. I prayed the same thing every night for years.

As the years went by, not eating dinner became a ritual of mine, and the beatings became part of that ritual. As a child I dreaded when it was time for my dad to come home from work. My mom would be in the kitchen cooking dinner. I would stand by her side, helping her. I enjoyed that time with my mom. When my dad wasn't home, she was relaxed and calm. She enjoyed cooking, and it always amazed me how much she knew about food. You could see her passion in the way she prepared dinner for her family.

My dad was hardworking, but even though he cared for his family by providing all the basic necessities, he was always drinking if he wasn't working. He was a full-blown, functioning alcoholic. He always had liquor around—bottles of it in our house, in the shed, and in the glovebox in his truck. He started drinking on his way home from work. As I watched the clock, I knew the time was getting closer to his arrival, closer to the ritual that had me stuck in a terrifying pattern. I hated that time of day since I worried about what could happen that night, and the dread was paralyzing.

As his truck pulled into the driveway, my mom would call the rest of my siblings to come down and set the table for dinner. We were all quiet when my dad walked in, trying to behave as best we could.

Part of setting the table was also making sure my dad had alcohol to drink. I would go out to the garage and grab a gallon-sized jug of Gallo red wine and bring it to the table. My dad would sit down at the head of the table, drinking, waiting to be served his meal. My dad would drink every night. He usually started in a good mood, but ultimately the alcohol would get the best of him, and the anger would come.

Dinner would be served, and then after a few bites my stomach would start aching again. My mom would encourage me to eat, but I just couldn't do it with the pain shooting through me. My siblings all would keep quiet, not wanting to make things worse.

"Eat your fucking dinner," my father would yell. "I work hard to put food on the table for you to eat, not to throw into the fucking garbage!" His anger would grow as he continued to yell until he'd had enough. Then he would stand up and take off his belt.

My dad's beatings were brutal. Immediately I would feel the sting of his belt on the first blow. My heart pounding, I would run as fast as I could up the stairs. I tried to get to my room, but most times he caught up to me before I could run inside and close the door. Then he would grab me by my leg and pull me down and start whipping me all over, his belt folded in half for more effect.

Kicking and screaming, I would fight back. "I hate you! Leave me alone!" My mind would start to wander, and I would mentally check out of the moment.

As he continued to hit me, I could feel the welt marks increasing in size and number. With each mark on my legs, my arms, and my face, I would feel worse, more ashamed of the evidence, the physical proof, that I was a bad child.

How will I be able to hide these tomorrow? That's what I would think to myself before breaking free and running to my bedroom to hide under my blanket, crouched in a fetal position with my back against the door. Each time, I knew it wasn't over. I would be terrified knowing he would be coming after me. I would hear his footsteps, heavier and louder as he got closer.

He would burst through the door. With the blanket still over me, I would jump onto the bed, but by that time he would have his belt lengthened so he could get a better reach across my bed. He would beat me, my blanket softening the blows somewhat, until he was too tired to hit any longer.

After the beating, my mom would put all the kids to bed to protect us from my dad's anger. After we said our prayers and she tucked us in, she'd go out to him. I could hear the yelling from my room until I finally drifted off to sleep, exhausted by our nightly ritual.

I was five years old when the nightmares started. I had horrible and traumatizing dreams about death. The same recurring and vivid stories involved me killing people or me dying a traumatic death. It was always *me* in the dreams, but my character was someone different every time.

In one dream, for example, I was a boy child standing at the top of a well. I looked down into pure blackness, and then suddenly I fell in. As soon as I entered the well, I woke up crying for my mother. I told her I'd had a nightmare, but I couldn't tell her the details of the dream because they were too powerful and I was afraid to tell her about them. She consoled me until I fell asleep.

Other nights I would wake up and sneak into my sister's bed while she was sleeping. Without waking her, I would curl up next to her and cry until I fell asleep. As I got older, the dreams became more violent. In one dream I was a soldier killing people with my bare hands on a battlefield. In another one I was a high school kid killing my classmates with a knife and cutting them up into pieces and then placing the parts into small metal cans so they wouldn't be found. In yet another, I was a young peasant woman living in the Middle Ages. I died running from a fire that engulfed me in its flames; I was alongside hundreds of other people killed as we fled for our lives from the village. The dreams became repeats, over and over—the same boy, the same soldier, the same peasant woman. Each time I would wake up, crying and wondering if they were real.

The dreams scared me beyond just their inherent terror. I blamed myself for having them. God had left me, I believed. I was a bad child. I deserved the nightmares. They were a curse the Devil had placed upon me. *None of my siblings have these nightmares, so it must be something I did.*

The dreams continued throughout my childhood. In high school I tried to write them down when I woke up to make them less scary, but that didn't help me overcome the fear I felt. I'd walk around in a daze all day thinking about what had happened. I tried to analyze them: *Why were they repeats? Why did they all end in death?*

I no longer believed in God by this time. I'd stopped praying when I was fourteen because as far as I could tell no one ever heard my prayers. God no longer existed for me. *So if God doesn't exist, then the Devil doesn't exist either, right?* I was confused in my spiritual beliefs. The more the reruns played in my mind, the more familiar they became, and over time they became a part of me.

I began to feel an intuition that the dreams were from past lives I had endured. It was a nagging feeling that wouldn't go away. I resonated with those characters. I *was* them. This change in my thinking made the nightmares easier to deal with. I'd still be shaken when I woke up, but I'd tell myself, *It's just a rerun.* Then I'd try to let it go.

I never told anyone about the nightmares. I wouldn't dare. I feared judgment from others for the horrible acts that I had committed during my past lives—not to mention that past lives in general were not a subject most people discussed at the time. The nightmares continued into my forties, and it wasn't until much later, when I went through my healing years, that I finally understood how much of an impact they'd had on me.

I have three siblings—two older sisters and a brother. My dad's relationship was uniquely different with each of us. For some reason I was usually the one getting hit. My dad beat me all the time for whatever reason he had that day: I didn't eat my dinner; I was fighting with my siblings; I didn't listen to whatever he had asked me to do. My hatred toward him continued to grow. I fought back, and because of my defiance he beat me almost daily.

Growing up with my siblings brought the usual family stuff. We fought and screamed and blamed one another when things went wrong. But despite our substantial differences, I have fond memories of my siblings growing up.

My oldest sister, Rosetta, is five years older than I am. I never saw my dad physically hit Rosetta, but he verbally abused her all the time. He told her she was stupid, just like he told my mom she was stupid. My dad put her down every chance he could, and I know it hurt her.

Even through her sadness because of my dad, Rosetta had a great sense of humor and loved to laugh. She was the one who would laugh so hard lemonade would pour out of her nose. Rosetta was the caretaker, and no matter what happened in our house, she always took care of us and made sure we had fun doing it.

Rosetta was a writer from a young age. She would write plays with parts for kids in the neighborhood to act out. One of my favorites was called *The Purple Ghost*. I loved my sister's plays. She typed her scripts on a manual typewriter and made several copies with carbon paper so she could hand them out to all of us who had roles in the play. We studied our lines feverishly and prepared for the big day.

Part of our job of being in the play was that we had to build our own sets too. We used cloth from the rolls of fabric my father brought home from his factory job, and Rosetta helped us make the costumes using my mom's sewing machine. We also made stage curtains by hanging the fabric on a clothesline. We lined up benches for the theater seats. After weeks of practicing, we invited the other neighborhood kids over to come see our play. We always knew whether the play was a hit based on the applause at the end. Everyone had fun, and that was because of my sister. Her plays were funny, mysterious, and very creative, just like she is.

Gina, who was the next oldest and just a year older than I was, could do no wrong. My dad made it known that she was his favorite, and he never laid a hand on her. We nicknamed her Princess. Still, Princess was fearful of my dad, so she followed all the rules in the house so as not to anger him, and she scolded us when we made him mad.

Princess was more serious than the rest of us. She was studious and a perfectionist. But in all her seriousness she was still part of our team. We played practical jokes on Princess all the time. My brother and I would hide in the hallway closet, each one of us on a shelf stuffed between the towels. We'd close the door tightly and wait until she came around the corner. We'd giggle and try to be as quiet as we could until we heard her coming. Slowly, her footsteps would get louder and louder until we knew she was close. "Now!" we'd whisper to each other and jump out of the closet.

She'd scream, and my brother and I would tumble to the floor laughing as we fell onto each other. "Stop it! Stop it! I hate when you do that!" she'd yell at us, but then her yelling would turn to laughter in the end.

Princess also had some serious obsessive-compulsive-disor-der issues with her food, and we took advantage of it. One day when she was making her lunch, we sat at the table and watched her patiently while she made her sandwich. Then we watched her count out her pretzels (twelve was her number) next to her sandwich and place her plate on the table while she went to get her drink.

"Don't touch my food," she said, watching us closely. But we couldn't help ourselves. As she poured her glass of soda, my brother stuck his finger in the sandwich while I breathed on her pretzels.

"C'mon, guys! I'm not eating that now!" After that she wouldn't touch it, and my brother and I got a free meal. We did this often, and we always got her meal. Secretly, I think Princess allowed us to do it so she could make us lunch without ever having to seem like she was doing us a favor.

I was the third child. Having had two girls already, my father really wanted a boy. He always took the opportunity to tell me that I was an accident and should have been a boy. I was antsy by nature and could never sit still. I was a tomboy. I wore shorts under my dresses and liked to run around, climb trees, and get dirty. My sisters were nothing like me, so I was thrilled when my brother came along. My brother, Carmelo, was born a few years after me. My dad was ecstatic. He was so proud to finally have a son. And I was just as excited.

I shared a room with Carmelo. One night when I was six, I woke up in the middle of the night to see him struggling to breathe. My mom was holding him, panicked.

"Frank, call the doctor!" she yelled. In those days doctors made house calls, and shortly after my dad called him, our doctor showed up at the house. I watched from the hallway as the doctor examined my brother.

"He's having an asthma attack," the doctor explained. I didn't know what asthma was at the time but could see it was very serious. From behind the door I watched, frozen. I prayed to God: *God, please don't let my brother die. Please, God, let him breathe.* I loved my baby brother so much and didn't want anything to happen to him.

The doctor gave Carmelo a shot of some kind, and after a while his breathing got better. After that night I worried about him all the time. Any kind of overactivity would trigger his asthma attacks, so we had to be careful that he didn't play too hard. The problem was that my brother *liked* to play hard. He was always running around and getting into trouble. Over the years his asthma got worse, so bad that his chest bone grew outward and you could see the outline of it pressing against his skin. Many nights our doctor would show up to give my brother a shot. Several times his attacks were so bad he would end up in the hospital in an oxygen tent so he could breathe. The more sickly my brother was, the more I hung out with him so I could watch over him. I made myself his protector, and the more I protected him, the more my dad blamed me for his sickness.

One hot, muggy day, my brother and I were running around the backyard. "I wish we could go swimming," he said. All of the neighborhood kids were at the local pool, but we were never allowed to go. "It's too expensive," my dad would say. Sometimes when my dad was watering the lawn with the sprinkler, he'd let us put our bathing suits on and run around. That day we both had the same idea.

Excited by our great idea, we ran into the house and put our bathing suits on. I turned on the sprinkler, and Carmelo ran to the edge of the water, careful not to get wet just yet. "C'mon, let's race!" he yelled.

I ran as quickly as I could and stood next to him. "Ready, set, go!" we yelled as we raced through the sprinkler to the other side of the yard. It was a tie. "Let's do it again!" And so we spent the afternoon running back and forth racing each other. It was always a tie since I never wanted to win against my brother.

We lost track of time. Suddenly our parents were home. My mom came running out of the back of the house. "Carmelo, what are you doing?" She ran up to him, grabbing him to dry him off with a towel. In that moment I could feel the terror building inside of me. I knew what was next.

Before I could think, my dad was coming out of the house and chasing after me. He grabbed my arm and held on tight while he whipped me with his belt.

"What are you doing? You know you're not supposed to get your brother excited!" he yelled as he hit me.

My mom put my brother down from her lap and came to my rescue again. I broke free and raced to my room to hide under my covers and wait for my dad to come up and finish his beating. As I lay there, I could hear him yelling, but his voice was still far away. I listened as closely as I could, and when I realized what was happening, my stomach lurched in pain and I wanted to vomit.

"You fucking stupid kid! What's wrong with you? You want to get sick? You want to go to the fucking hospital?" I could hear my dad's belt, but this time it wasn't me he was hitting. It was my brother.

"Frank, stop it. Stop it!" my mom frantically yelled.

Suddenly I heard my brother's little footsteps as he ran as fast as he could up the stairs. He ran into our room, slammed the door, and jumped onto his bed. The door flew open. My dad was in a rage. He was sweating and spitting as he yelled. My mom was right behind him, grabbing his arm and trying to stop him.

He took turns beating us, a few hits for me, a few for my brother. Back and forth and back and forth as I curled up under my covers, crying and waiting for it to be over.

"I don't want you playing with your brother. You're no good for him! You stay away from him," he yelled, his voice muffled through my covers.

"And you stay away from your sister! She's trouble. She's no good. You fucking stay away from her!" And with that he slammed the door as he left.

I crawled out from under the covers and climbed into my brother's bed. "It's OK, Carmelo. It's OK. It's going to be OK."

"I hate him," he said through his tears.

"I hate him too," I said.

Days like that only brought my brother and me closer and pushed my dad and my brother further apart.

We continued our adventures, most of them starting from our back porch. The porch was on the second floor and screened in, and it had a window that would open for the clothesline that ran to the opposite end of our yard. One afternoon on the porch, we came up with a plan to scare my mom. She was in the garden, and my brother and I climbed through that window, we both yelled for Mom to help, and then we jumped out the window to the grass. My mom came running from the garden toward us, screaming, "Oh my God!"—until she found us on the ground laughing.

"Carmelo, Marisa, what are you two doing? You're going to give me a heart attack. You two are wild ones!" And that was the nickname she gave us—"the wild ones." She never got mad at us. She enjoyed seeing my brother and me playing together.

I shared a bedroom with Carmelo until I was twelve. Then my dad split us up and put me in with my sisters. By then, my dad was beating my brother as much as he was beating me. I taught Carmelo to fight for himself. My dad forbade us from hanging out together, so we would sneak out of the house separately and then meet up somewhere so he wouldn't know we were together.

No matter what went down in the house, my siblings and I were a team, the prisoners against the prison guard. We protected one another during the bad times, even knowing the outcome would be painful. We would team up and make up stories that blamed Princess Gina if something was broken so no one would get my dad's wrath. We soothed one another when someone did.

One summer day my siblings and I were horsing around the house. One of us went flying through the wall and left a huge hole as big as a watermelon. "Dad is going to kill us for sure!" we said, panicked for fear of what the night would bring. In our fear we came up with a plan.

When Dad came home, Rosetta, Carmelo, and I hid in our rooms while Gina walked downstairs and slowly approached my dad.

I hope this works! I was shaking.

We were scared. We weren't sure he was going to believe us. And then Gina blurted out, "Dad, I was walking down the hallway, and I fell and my butt hit the wall, and now there's a hole in it."

My dad came up the stairs to look at the damage, and then he laughed. He laughed so hard at the thought of his favorite daughter falling through the wall. My siblings and I came out of our rooms to enjoy the moment. We laughed too and smiled at one another, relieved that our plan had worked, and no one had gotten in trouble that night.

My parents are from the same town. Both were raised on farms in the mountains of Sicily. My mom was the youngest of six children and the favorite of the family. Her parents and older brothers and sisters adored her, and she was surrounded by a loving family. Like all the women in her family, she learned to cook and sew. As a teenager, she taught sewing to the younger girls in her town. My mom was ahead of her time. She wore pants she'd made herself, and she bleached her hair blond. No one else behaved in this manner in the 1940s, not to mention in a small town in Sicily. She was also very particular about the type of man she wanted to marry. My mom would tell us how she'd had three marriage proposals by the time she was in her twenties, yet she'd turned them all down since none of them lived up to her expectations. As she repeated her story, I could always sense a feeling of regret that she hadn't accepted any of those proposals and had married my dad instead.

My dad's family lived near my mom's, and their families knew each other. He was the oldest of five siblings. My dad was a player—he had a reputation as a known womanizer and drinker. His parents wanted him to marry and settle down. They didn't like his partying ways. My parents were the same age, both twenty-six—which was old to be single in those days—when their parents got together and decided they should get married.

My dad thought my mom was stuck up, and he didn't want to marry her. My mom didn't like my dad's womanizing and drinking and said she wouldn't marry him unless he stopped both of those behaviors. My dad's parents had already moved to America and were living in Pennsylvania, where my grandfather was a coal miner. My mother knew that my dad was moving there, and the thought of moving to America was exciting to her. It was not a match made in heaven, but with their families' pressure, they agreed to get married.

When they were ready to travel to America, my sister Rosetta was nine months old, and my mother was pregnant with a second child. My father was not happy about the pregnancy. By this time my dad's parents had made their way to New York. My mom and dad were planning to settle there, along with his sister and brother-in-law, to be with his family. My dad explained to my mom that she couldn't have the baby in America because they wouldn't have insurance and they couldn't afford to deliver the baby. With support and pressure from his family, my dad gave my mom two options: stay behind and have the baby while he took my sister to America without her or have an abortion.

My mom was conflicted. She was of strong Catholic faith, and an abortion was against her beliefs. But she also couldn't bear to leave her only daughter. She was only one month pregnant, and if she waited until her baby was born it would be another year before she could travel again. They already had their travel papers, and it would be difficult to get another chance to arrange for new papers.

The procedure was simple. They would make an incision in the womb and wait for her to miscarry. It would take about a week, the doctors told her, and it was exactly one week before her boat was to depart. My mom spent nine days in the infirmary aboard the boat—the entire trip—hemorrhaging from her abortion. Those horrific days marked the beginning of her resentment toward my father.

My mom has told me this story many times, and it's heartbreaking each time I hear it. Her marriage to my father wasn't love at first sight but a marriage of convenience.

Arriving in America, my father immediately got a job in a local factory that dyed large reams of fabrics, and he remained there until he retired. Twelve days after their arrival, my mother—still bleeding from her miscarriage—took a job as a seamstress working at a factory making coats. She moved from the coat factory to a curtain factory before taking a few years off to raise us kids, and then she went back to work as a cook in a mental health facility. Neither one of my parents finished school past the eighth grade, but together they purchased several real estate investments over the years and altogether owned nine apartment buildings.

My mother's family never left Sicily. She missed her family immensely. Whenever she spoke of her parents and siblings, she would resonate with joy. Her grandparents were cheesemakers and had a shop where they sold homemade cheeses with the milk from their farms. Her parents had a nut and olive tree farm, and her brothers were sheepherders. She kept in touch by phone and letters. Each month my mother's family would send her a care package from their farms to remind her of home. I was always excited to get the large brown box with a brown rope tied around it. My mother would cut the rope and tear open the box, and out would pour fresh nuts, hard cheeses, and olives, right from Sicily! It was like Christmas for me and my siblings as we hovered over the box, waiting for its contents to spill out onto the floor.

When I was twelve, we took a trip to see her family. They lived high on a mountaintop. Their house was very small, with a cement floor. They used an outdoor oven and had an outhouse for a bathroom. My uncle built an indoor shower for us when he found out we were coming. The shower had a large metal bucket on the roof, similar to what a horse would drink out of, and my uncle had to fill the bucket for us to take a shower. Inside, my parents threw all four of us kids into the shower at the same time to get clean. The water was not hot, but at least we had some degree of the convenience we'd grown up with in America!

We drank milk that was fresh from the cow and then boiled on the stove. We made pasta every day and cooked on the outdoor oven. I had just gotten braces before our trip, and I recall how many local people remarked that I had metal in my mouth—they'd never seen braces before.

The trip was the only time my mom ever saw her family in all her years of living in America, and on that trip, I saw how much love her family had for one another. I wanted that for our family since ours seemed broken in comparison. My mother had a strong foundation back in her hometown, and she'd lost all of that when she married my dad. I always felt bad for what she'd given up, and it made me appreciate her so much more. She was alone with no support system, raising her kids in a foreign world with her alcoholic and abusive husband.

All of my dad's family had made it to America, and they were very different from my mom's family. I found our family get-togethers depressing as there was always a lot of fighting. My aunts had a lot of anger and resentment toward my dad because he had physically beaten them on a regular basis growing up. Everyone talked about my dad's anger and drinking, and no one was spared during his rages in response. In those moments his siblings yelled back, and the fights usually escalated, with my aunts eventually storming out in tears.

It was during one of those get-togethers that I overheard my dad tell a story about a dead man in the mountains. I had heard a small portion of the story and wanted to know more. The next morning, I saw my dad sitting in our yard with a wet handkerchief over his head drinking a beer. He had been in our garden all morning, and, hot and sweaty, he'd sat down to take a break.

"Dad, tell me the story about the man in the mountains."

"*Parcesepare*, when I was a young man, I was working in the mountains, and after a long day, I started to head back home. From a distance I saw a man, sitting by a tree. I thought to myself, 'It's hot—he must be taking a break.' As I walked closer I saw that the man was slumped over with his head down. I walked up to him and asked him if he was OK, and the man said nothing to me. I bent down and put my hand on his shoulder, and he fell over. He was dead!"

The first time my dad told us the story of the dead man in the mountains, I believed him, but after hearing this story several times over the years, I started to notice the smile, the one that instilled fear in me, in the telling of his story.

"Marisa, he was dead, and I went home and told my parents that he was dead." That smile in the last part of his story made me question what I was hearing. And I can't remember the rest of the story since my mind would wander as I looked at him intensely, wondering the truth of it all. I always felt part of the story was missing. *Could his storytelling be a partial confession of a wrongdoing or a boasting of his achievements?* I was convinced it was the latter.

On the weekends, my dad would drive an hour to upstate New York in the middle of the night and go to live animal auctions in the morning. When he'd return, he'd come back with a cow, a pig, or a goat. My brother and I would get so excited and run down to the garage so we could pet the animal while it was still alive as my dad prepared for his task.

For the remainder of the morning, my brother and I would watch him slaughter, prepare, and freeze the animal we had just been petting. Watching my dad's ritual of slicing the animal's throat was sad and sickening at the same time. I felt sorry for the animal that had just brought me so much joy to pet while my emotions hardened for the man who was doing the killing. He loved it. He was proud of it. He loved to watch us be disgusted by it. Since we were in the suburbs, he always slaughtered the animals with the garage door closed, but when he was done, he'd open the garage door and hose the blood down the driveway into the street. It wasn't until I was older that I wondered what the neighbors thought of this.

When my dad wasn't working, he loved to go hunting. He hunted deer and small game and would go on weeklong hunting trips and come home with the occasional deer. At home he would go into the local woods and kill small animals such as rabbits, pheasants, and squirrels to feed the family. We raised chickens, pigeons, and rabbits, and my siblings and I had the chore of cleaning their pens. I loved caring for the animals, feeding them from boxes of lettuce we'd find in dumpsters behind the grocery stores and giving them rinds from our watermelons. I loved being with the animals. I always petted the animals and talked to them while I was in their coops, but I tried not to get attached since they always made their way to the dinner table. One afternoon my brother and I came home from school and walked into the garage, only to see a bushel basket filled with at least a dozen skinned rabbits. My brother and I just stood there, saddened and wondering the same thing: Which one's Fluffy?

My mom had been a strict vegetarian since she was a young girl. Growing up on a farm in Sicily and seeing the regular slaughtering of animals made her not want to eat them. But as a wife and mother, she would dutifully help my dad take apart an animal, carefully putting all the ingredients into separate bowls to be used for a future meal and leaving nothing to waste.

In our refrigerator we always had bowls of blood, brains, skulls with eyeballs, and other "parts unknown." *chef Anthony Bourdain would be proud.* The blood would be congealed and fried. Brains were apparently good scrambled with some eggs, and skulls made a great stew that would bring a smile to my dad's face as he sucked on the skull and eyeballs during dinner, knowing it all made us want to vomit with disgust. He was proud of his hunting achievements, and my parents were the perfect example of the "hunter-gatherer" definition. The look on my dad's face when sucking that skull always made me feel sick to my stomach. As he held the skull with both hands, the juices would spill down his chin, and he'd look right at us. Enjoying the taste of his meal and proud of his kill, a smile would emerge from his mouth full of meat as his eyes grew dark.

"Do you want some?" he'd ask us, knowing the answer. There was something about those eyes. They were pure evil, and the fear I felt made my skin crawl. *He's sick in the head. He's not normal. What the hell is that anyway?* Was it a squirrel, a rabbit, or even our cat? I could never be sure. We had a lot of cats growing up, strays that we'd bring home and become part of our family. They were both indoor and outdoor cats that would come and go at their leisure.

My dad hated the cats. He would kick them out of his way and yell, "Those fucking cats! I'm going to skin them and cook them and make a stew out of them!"

Then the anger would turn into laughter as we pleaded with him. "Not the cats! No, don't eat the cats!" I never got too close to the cats because at some point they always disappeared for good. When they did, my siblings and I would whisper to one another, "Did Dad eat the cat? Is that the cat for dinner?" We never knew for sure. Was dinner that night his way of showing us that our life was a game to him? A game where he made the rules and he always won?

Because my dad hunted, we had two beagles called Snoopy and Beam. The beagles did not live in our house but outside in a doghouse. My brother and I liked to help my dad train the dogs to hunt. Holding a vial of blood that my dad would save from one of his kills, I'd walk around and slowly drip the blood, making a trail around the yard. Once my job was complete, we'd take one of the dogs and start him at the beginning of the trail. We'd follow him to the end, slowly nudging him back when he was distracted. I liked the dogs, but over the years I started to see a similar pattern with the dogs that I had with the cats. They disappeared.

The first time Snoopy disappeared, my dad came home with another beagle. My dad still spoke very little English, and he wanted to keep the dog's name easy to remember, so he named the beagle Snoopy Two. Shortly after, Beam didn't come home from one of my dad's hunting trips, and my dad came home with another dog, who was properly named Beam Two. You would think with a beagle's lifespan of twelve to fifteen years, we would never get past Snoopy Two, but that wasn't the case in our house.

I was in high school when my dad returned from a hunting trip without our dog, Snoopy Four.

"Where's Snoopy?" I asked.

My mom looked at my dad, and in her eyes I saw anger and disappointment.

My dad looked at her, and then me, and crouched down as if in the moment, hiding between the bushes, looking for prey. "I was in the woods," he said, "waiting for a rabbit, and then I saw one. He jumped right in front of me! I said, 'Snoopy, go get him!' But he's stupid, that dog. He just sat there. He wouldn't hunt."

Then my dad slowly stood up and held up his arms as if he was holding a gun. He took aim toward the floor and said, "He wouldn't hunt, so I shot him. Pow!" Then he started laughing, with that smile on his face. He'd won against the dog, and he was proud of it.

I was in shock, watching his reenactment as if I had witnessed it myself.

"Dad, how could you?" I said. "Is that what happened to our other dogs?"

He looked at me, still laughing. "The fucking dog is stupid. He wouldn't hunt!"

That week my father went to get another dog at the ASPCA, where he always got our dogs, but this time they wouldn't give him one.

The realization that my dad had been killing our dogs was shocking but not surprising. Still, the more I heard, the more fearful I became of this man. With each new story of his unraveling, the more he added to his vocabulary when he was beating us and the more terror he instilled in me.

As I grew older, I'd run out of the house when he was beating me instead of to my room. I would disappear for a few hours until I could sneak back in when he was passed out asleep, but he always heard me come back in. Like a predator waiting on its dying prey, belt in hand, he would find me in my bed under my blanket and get his last hits in.

I would sleep like that all night, with my head under the covers, knowing that he might return at any time to continue with his rage. While I lay there, I could hear him yell through the house, "I'm *king* of this *fucking* house! I'm going to fucking shoot you in your sleep and bury you in the fucking backyard with the fucking dogs!"

I was terrified and stayed as small and quiet as I could. Some nights when I was brave enough, I would sneak out from under the covers and put a chair up against my door handle to keep him from reentering. Then I'd climb back into the safety of my bed and cry myself to sleep.

Of course I believed he would kill me, and why wouldn't I? I had seen him kill many things. Killing was part of his nature, and he never showed remorse or compassion for the animals he killed. Killing was part of his family, as my dad liked to remind us: "My uncle tried to straighten out his family for years, and one day he killed all seven of them—every fucking one of them! But he was stupid because he killed himself after. I'll fucking kill you all, and then I'll live in peace!"

When you're a kid and you're fighting a fight you know you can't win, a few things happen that both make you stronger and break you down at the same time. When you live in fear for your life, it makes you angry, and when you're consumed with fear and anger, your survival instincts kick in. My attacker was my dad, and I fought back against him as much as a young child could. But because I was powerless, I took my vengeance out against others around me.

My first instinct was defense. I was always on the defense trying to beat my dad. This carried over into everything I did, especially school. Gym class was especially a challenge for me because, back in those days, we had gym class every day, and you had to change into your gym uniform. Our uniform was a red-and-white-striped jumpsuit with shorts and short sleeves. I refused to put it on. While everyone else was changing into uniforms in the locker room, I took my seat on the gym floor and waited for the rest of the class to join me. It wasn't that I didn't want to wear the uniform—I couldn't care less about the striped outfit, and everyone else had to wear the same one. It was that putting it on would show the welts I had on my arms and legs, and I was not going to show those marks to anyone.

So as everyone walked into the gym and took a place seated on the floor, I sat down in my street clothes, arms tense, adrenaline running its course through my veins, waiting for battle with whomever should challenge me.

"Why aren't you in your gym clothes?" my teacher would ask. "Go back in and change like the rest of the kids."

"*No!* I'm not changing. Fuck you." My dad cursed a lot, and I'd learned to use that same language, so powerful, as my only weapon in battle. Off to detention I went, satisfied and proud of myself that I had defended myself in battle.

My next instinct was to fight, and I had a lot of fight in me. I wanted to physically punch something—but what? Or who?

When I was in the first grade, I was sent to the principal's office for fighting with a boy in my class. I was angry at him, and I had scratched down the entire front of his chest with both of my hands so hard that he bled through his shirt. It doesn't matter why I did it—that was my first memory of becoming a bully.

I never realized I was a bully until I was an adult healed from my anger. No one labeled me as such back then since we didn't label bullies, but I was the definition of what would be called a bully in today's terms.

I bullied a lot of kids throughout my school years. There was my neighbor John. He took karate lessons, so to prove that I could beat him up even though I never took karate, I did, regularly. I'd start a fight with him for no reason, kick over his bike while he was walking it home from school, and then berate him just for being him.

In high school there was Robert. He was very smart, a nerd, and his locker was next to mine. He was sloppy and always had papers spilling out from his locker. I took every chance I had to grab the stack of stuff piled in his locker from the top and pour it out onto the floor like water through a breaking dam, creating havoc for everyone around. I poked him with pencils in class and taunted him for his looks.

I called kids mean names: fat, stupid, retarded, ugly. When I got older, it was douchebag, whore, slut. I fought anyone for any reason. I'm only five foot one, but anyone of any size was a target. This was my way of expressing my anger and controlling my circumstances. By beating up other people and abusing them verbally, I was surviving. I was no longer powerless.

I also fought in the name of my brother. He was small and weak from his severe asthma, and kids teased him because of it.

I was walking home from school one day when a friend came running up the street calling my name. "Marisa, stop! Come back—some kids are beating up your brother!"

My heart raced, and I could feel it pounding in my chest as I ran back down to the school as fast as I could. Once I got there, I saw two kids hovering over my brother. One of them had his knee pushed into my brother's back so he couldn't get up while the other grabbed his hair and pushed his head into the dirt. I could see the dust flying up around my brother's face. *Oh fuck—he's going to have an asthma attack!*

When I got close enough, I grabbed the kid with his knee on my brother and pulled him back by his shirt; then I punched him twice in the face and knocked him down to the ground. Then I grabbed the other kid and pulled him by his hair and swung him around until he fell to the ground. I pushed his face into the dirt and smashed it over and over into the dirt just like he had done to my brother.

"Run, Carmelo, run!" I yelled as I continued to beat up the boys. My brother ran up the street. When I was confident the boys weren't going to win this fight, I yelled, "Don't ever touch my fucking brother again!" And with one last kick I took off.

While I couldn't control my brother's asthma, I tried to protect him generally from external harm. I took him under my wing and made myself his guardian. I taught him how to be me—tough and thick-skinned against the kids who teased him for his frailty and, most importantly, against my dad. Messing with my brother meant getting the wrath of me in return.

My brother was eleven when he was playing football with some of the older boys on the block one day. He was not allowed to play with those kids because of his asthma, but as

I've mentioned, my brother was stubborn and loved being active. I was at a neighbor's house and wasn't home when one of the kids he was playing with came running up the street and rang our doorbell to say that my brother had broken his leg while playing.

By the time I got the news, the ambulance had already taken my brother away. The kids in the neighborhood all knew my dad, and I could feel their fear as they told me the story. "We ran to your house as fast as we could and rang the doorbell," they said. "Your dad answered, and we said, 'Mr. Scaglione, Carmelo broke his leg. You need to take him to the hospital.'"

Hearing the news, my dad jumped into his truck and drove down to the schoolyard and parked his truck on the field. He walked up to my brother, lying there with a broken leg, and started kicking and beating him right there and then.

"I told you not to play with these fucking kids!" he yelled, kicking Carmelo multiple times as hard as he could while my brother lay there helpless.

My arms tensed up as I heard the story. "Fuck! *God fuck-kkk!*" And then I began to cry.

I need to get us out of there.

In that moment, I wanted to disappear and take my brother with me. I was only fourteen. I knew I couldn't go anywhere. I was trapped in this miserable existence with the Devil as my father. I walked upstairs into my parents' bedroom and stared at my dad's side of the bed. With as much phlegm as I could cough up, I lifted his pillow, spit on the sheets below, then dropped his pillow back down on the bed.

My brother spent an entire month in the hospital with his leg in traction, broken in two places. I had failed to protect him from my dad that day. How badly was he hurt from the game, and how much of his injury was caused by my father? My mom spent every day in the hospital, and I went with her whenever I could. I had to go. I had to show him that I would always be there for him.

Back in those days, there wasn't much help for a kid like me. I was labeled a troublemaker in school. I spent countless hours in the principal's office or detention. My parents never asked me about homework, never went to school conferences, and couldn't understand why I was causing so much trouble. "All you have to do is listen to your dad," my relatives would tell me. They talked about me behind my back, and I listened. I heard what a bad kid I was—"the black sheep of the family," they called me.

My mom didn't think I was bad, but she wanted me to listen. She couldn't understand why I had to break the rules all the time. My siblings and I asked her why she didn't leave our dad, but she said she didn't know where to go. She felt trapped. "If I leave, he will kill me and take you kids. I don't want him to take you kids because then I can't protect you."

After one of my dad's beatings when I was sixteen, I called a friend of mine whose father was a cop and told her about the abuse. "I can't live there anymore. I can't take it," I said. She took me to her house, and after I spoke with her father about my situation, he agreed to help me. He made a phone call, and the police went to my house to talk to my dad.

At the same time, a car came to pick me up and take me to a group home to speak with a counselor and see if I wanted to stay there. I sat in a room with an older man who asked me to tell him my story. *Finally, I'm free*, as I spilled my horrors to this man. And then something happened that surprised me.

"Your father is just being a good parent," the man said. "You need to listen to him. You're not a good kid. You're a troublemaker. You need to be reformed." The year was 1981, and hitting children was an acceptable form of punishment.

This stranger, who knew nothing about me, was telling me it was my fault that I was getting beatings and that I was the one who was bad. He offered to put me in a group home for troubled kids like me.

"Fuck you," I said. "You don't know anything about me!" I got up and walked out. *I was not a bad kid. I was the victim! My father was the bad one.*

There were no consequences for my dad. I went home that night and got my usual beating.

Being told you're the bad kid most of your life makes you start to question your values. I thought I was a good kid. I thought I knew wrong from right. But if God wasn't listening to me and everyone around me thought I was the bad kid, the black sheep, then maybe that *was* me.

Angry and frustrated about my situation, I felt hopeless. I was surviving as best I could under the circumstances, but my heart ached for some kind of normalcy. I was confused and giving up. *Fuck everyone. Fuck life. Fuckkkkkk!*

When I hear about a bully today in school, I feel for that kid and hope that someone is helping him or her with whatever horrors of a home life that child might be experiencing.

I wanted to belong and fit in. Being a kid is a time for child-hood innocence, for fun and playing games. There were many American traditions involving kids that I wanted to participate in whenever I could, but being raised in an immigrant family, I found that sometimes our traditions differed quite a bit. That's not to say that is the case for all immigrant families, but it was definitely the case in mine.

One American tradition that was big when I was growing up, and still is today, is block parties—all your neighbors getting together so the parents can barbecue, drink, and chill while the kids run around and play. Our neighbors had a lot of block parties—only our family did not participate. My parents forbade it. On those nights my siblings and I were outcasts, yearning to join the other kids. We at least had one another. We looked out the window, listening to the kids playing, running around way past their bedtimes, and enjoying the nighttime. We watched as if we were watching a television show, laughing and saying to one another, "I wish we could go outside."

At Christmas, we didn't wake up to presents under the tree. Sometimes we'd have gifts under the tree from relatives, but Santa didn't visit our house. I asked my dad once, "Why doesn't Santa come to our house?" Without looking up from the television, he answered, "Because we don't have a fireplace."

When we were older, he would give us a card with fifty dollars in it, but he would sign only his name. He wouldn't include our mother's on the card because he was "the one who made the money," he explained. My mom would sit there in awe and hurt when we asked her why she didn't get us a present.

My dad also forbade us from participating in the typical childhood rituals of going out for Halloween and setting off fireworks in the street on the Fourth of July. These were traditions we enjoyed only after we had waited until we were teenagers, when we could experience them on our own. We always asked our parents to go trick-or-treating or celebrate the Fourth, but we never got an explanation as to why we couldn't join in the fun.

My dad just said no, and my mom knew better than to disagree.

At school, we weren't allowed to join sports teams or clubs. We had to come home after school—or at least get there before our parents got home from work. "This sucks. I fucking hate my dad," I would say as my mantra. Our house was our prison from which we watched the world go by. We were different, I was different, and it was my dad's fault. As my anger grew, so did my resentment toward my dad. I was a victim of this house, my family, my life. My curse, the self-inflicted curse of being a victim, was forming.

BY THE TIME I WAS in my teen years, I did everything I could do to escape the demon living in my house. I stopped talking to God since there was no one listening to my pleas. My mind was tortured with the visions of killings in my sleep and the death of my soul over and over again as I lay down to sleep each night. I was angry, very angry, and all alone. I thought about suicide often because the world was a negative place and I no longer wanted to be a part of it.

As I sat in my room, staring at the walls, I'd start to get angry about my prison sentence. If my mom was at home, I'd start yelling that I couldn't stand being there and that I had to leave. She'd beg me to stay. "Please, Marisa. If you go, your father is going to get angry. Don't do that to yourself."

"Fuck him. Fuck this house. I'm leaving!" I'd reply. I knew it hurt her, but I couldn't stay. There were no cell phones yet, so my mom had no way of reaching me. She worried and prayed every night that I was safe wherever I was. If I was only gone for a night or two, I could get away with it. My mom knew my dad would kill me, so she would cover for me, telling him when he came home from work that I had already eaten dinner and was in my room.

At the age of fourteen I started smoking cigarettes and pot. By the time I was fifteen, I had added LSD, mushrooms, whippets, speed, and cocaine to my repertoire. Anything I could get my hands on I took. Sometimes I sold small amounts of pot and cocaine so I could get free drugs for myself. And I drank a lot.

Alcohol was easy to get since our house was always stocked with liquor—whiskey, vodka, bourbon, wine, you name it. Drinking a highball was common in my house, and we were all allowed to imbibe. Only my mother abstained from drinking.

Growing up with an alcoholic and parents who had grown up in a country where drinking at all ages was legal, alcohol was always part of my life. When my sisters and brother and I were little, my dad would frequently give us money to walk to the liquor store to buy a bottle of whiskey and cigarettes—you could do that in the old days. As a treat we could have a shot when we returned.

On hot summer days my dad would sit outside on the front stoop drinking a cold beer. I'd go out and sit next to him, knowing that he would offer me a sip. When the can was empty, he'd ask me to go inside and get us another one, and we'd drink that one together as well. My dad would talk about the work he had done in the yard or the troubles he had with us kids. He was vulnerable while I listened. I would comment on any topic he was willing to share, except when it came to us kids. That would always turn into a fight if I was allowed to share my opinion on those matters.

When it was cold outside and we'd spent the afternoon shoveling snow, my dad would reward us with Jack Daniel's. He'd pour a few shot glasses and hand them out to me and my siblings. I always took my glass, looking forward to it. Then he'd look at us with a big smile on his face and say, "This will warm you up." It was sharp, and it burned my throat, but upon hearing the joy in my dad's laughter as I puckered my mouth and cringed, I would innocently ask, "Can I have another one?" And my dad would oblige.

Wine at dinner was allowed for any of us who wanted it. I liked the buzz, but more than anything I liked anything I could do to make my dad like me. Times when I shared his love of drinking were the only good memories I had of my dad at the time. Alcohol, the poison that brought out his dark side and drove a wedge between us, was ironically the only catalyst that brought us together. As I got older, I got used to the taste, but more importantly I got used to the buzz. I'd sneak a glass of wine or a shot of whiskey whenever no one was around to catch me. What I enjoyed most about it was how it made me not feel anything.

Those bonding moments with my dad were fleeting. His anger would eventually surface. I became more dependent on drugs and alcohol and didn't care if anyone in my house knew it. My fights with my dad grew worse, and our exchanges were heated.

As I'd walk into the house high on something, way past my curfew, my dad would greet me screaming, "You're out with your friends doing drugs—this is *my* house. I make the fucking rules here!"

And as he'd whip out his belt, I'd run up to my room and yell back at him, "Fuck you! You don't fucking own me. *Fuck you!*" I'd then place my chair against my door.

The yelling echoed across the house, and I'd cry in my room. When I heard my dad's snoring loudly from my room, I would know he'd passed out from drinking. With my parents asleep, I'd quietly enter their room. My dad's pants would lay neatly over a chair in the corner. I'd walk slowly to his pants and stick my hand in to reach his wallet. I'd grab a few twenties and then lay his pants down again and go out.

My mom knew I stole money from my dad. I even stole some coins she had been saving that were collectibles. She confronted me about it. She knew if my dad found out he would beat me, but I didn't care.

"He beats me anyway," I told her.

My mom and I had an interesting relationship. She did everything she could to protect us kids from our dad, but I was the one who needed her protection the most. She lied for me when

I wasn't at dinner. She covered for me when I wasn't home. And she pleaded with me to stop. My mom understood the pain and anger that I felt—she felt it too. She wanted me to listen so this man she married wouldn't hurt me, yet something inside me couldn't do it.

We talked about it a lot. "I worry about you doing drugs. I don't know where you are or who you are with. I love you and don't want to see you get hurt," she'd say.

"Mom, I love you too, but I can't stay. I'm sorry."

As much as I loved my mom, her words escaped me emotionally. I didn't think about what she was going through; nor did I care at the time. If my mom wouldn't leave my dad, that was for her to deal with, but I didn't have to live by his rules. Mentally I checked out of my family—out of sight, out of mind. I left my siblings to deal with the wrath of my dad whenever I took off or he caught me doing drugs. The only one I cared about was myself, and whenever I could, I took my brother along with me. It was time to live life on my terms.

I snuck out of the house after my parents went to sleep every chance I could. Sometimes I'd be gone for days at a time, sleeping at friends' houses. Drinking, smoking, and doing drugs—anything to escape my family and myself. When I was high, I was having fun. It numbed me from the pain I felt inside.

On one trip I left for an entire week. I went to Wildwood, New Jersey, with my girlfriends to hang out at the beach. I didn't tell anyone where I was going or how long I would be gone. I drank and partied all week, only thinking of myself. I didn't bother to think about how much I must have worried my mom, and when I returned, she didn't speak to me for about the same length of time as I'd been gone. It was the first and only time she got really mad at me. After that I made it a habit to call her at work whenever I would be gone for more than a few days.

Coming back home was always painful—arms tensed up, fists clenched as I walked in, braced for my beating. The beatings were tough and painful, but it was worth it for a few days of freedom away from this man who despised everything about me.

Growing up in New York, just outside of Manhattan, had its perks, one of them being the many concert venues across the tri-state area. I went to a lot of concerts, and I kept track—in fact, by the time I was in my twenties, I had been to over 120 shows. Concerts were a great place to do drugs, and I was always high smoking marijuana, snorting cocaine, and dropping LSD and doing mushrooms. Comfortably numb, just the way I liked it.

Friday and Saturday nights there were big school parties. My high school was a large public school with 6,000 kids. There were always several parties going in the area with different groups of friends. I'd buy myself a bottle of vodka and a carton of orange juice and drink rum and Cokes and Boone's Farm wine. I'd drink until I passed out.

The drinking age was eighteen, but no one checked IDs in 1980. Everyone was welcome, even if you were only fifteen. My girlfriends and I would regularly go into Manhattan and hit the clubs: The Blue Note, The Peppermint Lounge, dance clubs, night clubs, and bars where we saw famous musicians such as David Bowie, Clarence Clemons, Roomful of Blues, and Buddy Guy. We went out most nights of the week, even on school nights, dancing to eighties music, doing unlimited shots, getting into fights with other girls just because we didn't like their looks, and drinking until the sun came up.

We took buses to get around, and we hitchhiked, sometimes an hour or more away, drunk as hell, shoes in hand, wanting to get somewhere to sleep. We didn't care that people like Ted Bundy or Son of Sam were out there. We were invincible. No one would mess with us! The details are gone, and the memories are dusty, but I do remember I had a lot of fun. That was my escape. It was all one big distraction, anything to keep from going home to my own personal prison and the prison guard from hell.

By the age of fifteen, I was one of "the burnouts," a label for the bad kids at school who partied and smoked cigarettes and marijuana just outside the doors on school grounds. I had a lot of friends, and there was always someone to hang out with. I was up for anything.

One day after school, I was with my friend Laura, and we decided to take the bus to the mall and go shopping. I had a curfew to come home directly after school, but I wasn't following my dad's rules by that time. On the way to the mall, Laura told me that she never paid for anything, that she stole whatever she wanted. "It's easy," she said. "I'll teach you."

As we walked around the mall, she spotted a store and said that was our target. "Watch me and see how I do it," she said, and we walked inside. It was a store that carried various items, such as clothing, trinkets, and jewelry. She looked at me, and her eyes looked downward toward a bracelet and then back to me. Slowly she grabbed the bracelet. She slid it into her coat pocket, then casually walked out. I looked around and saw that no one was paying attention to us. My eyes spotted a gold necklace—it was pretty and sparkling. I didn't need the necklace, but the rush of what I was about to do was exhilarating. I grabbed the necklace and clenched it in my hand, then put my hand in my pocket and walked out.

Laura was excited. "Did you do it? Did you get anything?" I pulled my hand out of my pocket and dangled the necklace in front of her. We both smiled—"cool," we said—and went back home on the bus. We were walking home when suddenly a blue pickup truck slowed down and stopped in front of us. It was my dad.

"Where have you been? I've been looking all over for you. Get in the fucking truck!" I got in, and he left my girlfriend standing there by herself. My dad yelled at me the entire way home. As soon as we pulled up to the house, I jumped out of the truck and ran as fast as I could to my room, with him following me and hitting me along the way. After my dad left my room, I pulled the necklace out of my pocket and stared at it. It was my secret. I opened my dresser drawer and closed it shut with the necklace inside.

After a few days, I couldn't stop thinking about the necklace. I felt bad about taking it. Even though I no longer believed in God, I didn't want to take any chances of not getting into heaven in case I was wrong. So that weekend I went to confession. Confession is a religious practice of the Catholic Church in which you go to church and tell a priest all of your sins in order to absolve yourself. Usually the priest sits in a confessional booth where he can't see your face. I never knew why that was, but I suppose it makes it easier to tell your sins to someone you can't see.

When I was a kid, I had my confession memorized. I used the same one every time: "Bless me, Father, for I have sinned. I'm sorry I didn't listen to my parents. I'm sorry I fought with my brothers and sisters." I wasn't sorry, but I had to say something, and that was all I could think of.

This time, I walked into the church, and on this particular day, for some reason, the priests were sitting in pews instead of the confessional. *Ugh.* I had a pit in my stomach. I walked up to the priest and knelt down beside him.

"Bless me, Father, for I have sinned. I'm sorry I didn't listen to my parents, and I fought with my brothers and sisters," I said.

He replied, "Is that all of your sins, my child?"

I hesitated, nervous for what I was about to reveal. Then I spoke. "I stole a necklace." OK, I had done it. I knelt quietly, waiting to be absolved. But when he spoke again, his voice sounded deep and heavy, with a sternness that hadn't been there before.

"The Lord's commandment says thou shalt not steal. You broke a commandment … "

I could no longer pay attention to his words—only his voice—as I heard the harsh judgment in his tone. As he spoke, my mind raced with thoughts of anger. *He doesn't know anything about me. He's just a priest. Fuck this.*

"But I gave it back!" I lied. I lied to the priest so I wouldn't have to hear his lecture.

His tone softened. "Your penance is seven Hail Marys and one Our Father. You may go in peace." It wasn't the last time I stole, but it was the last time I entered a church for many, many years.

I was making poor choices on a regular basis, and I no longer cared about the consequences. In my first year of high school I had aced algebra and Italian, getting 100 percent on my state exams. By my third year, I was drinking before school every morning and getting high between classes. My teachers saw the change in me and called me out on it. After failing an exam in Italian class, my teacher lectured me in front of the class about my drug use and how it was affecting my grades. I stood up, climbed over my desk, and said, "Fuck you" as I walked out the door. When a girl died in gym class while running the bases during a softball game, the next week my girlfriend and I pretended to do the same during our class, sending our teacher into the school in tears while we were sent to detention.

I was brazen and tough and making a name for myself in school. I fought the girls who were "popular," the ones who dated the jocks, just because I could. My burnout friends loved me for it. On the outside I exuded confidence. I was an adventurer, a survivor, a little bit crazy to some. On the inside I was an emotional mess.

I had a lot of close friends who knew about my home life and did whatever they could to protect me. They let me sleep over at their homes and even came to my rescue. If he wouldn't let me leave, they would yell at my dad from the street that he couldn't keep me there as his prisoner. But I kept the turmoil in my mind a secret to them. They didn't know about the nightmares. They didn't know the fear I endured going to sleep thinking I might succumb to my dad's shotgun. They didn't know that I was drinking and getting high even when I was alone. And they didn't know that I did it to escape my own head and numb the pain because when I wasn't high, I was often thinking about ending my life.

I thought about suicide a lot. *Should I take a lot of drugs, drive off a cliff, or slit my wrists?* It was freeing to think about it since dying was the only way I knew how to escape the mental mindfuck in my head. My thoughts exhausted me.

Each morning I woke up dreading the same routine. Waking up after a nightmare, shaken with the images from my sleep, I would write down my dream, my mind trying to figure out what it meant. The sadness and depression would then kick in from what I had witnessed the night before. My dad would already be gone to work, and my mom would be getting ready to go. I would sneak downstairs and pour myself a double shot of whiskey and take a swig. *I fucking hate my life.* I would head out the door and down the street, smoking a joint as I walked to school.

My mind would be at ease as I met up with my friends before classes. We would look at one another and ask, "Should we go in today or not?" Going to school meant having to hear bullshit from my teachers, so I would typically opt out. I would spend the day with friends drinking and smoking—a great distraction that made me happy.

Dinner would roll around—time to head home. My friends would drop me off at the end of the street so my dad wouldn't see them. Anger would kick in as I walked up the block, and I would want to scream. Fear and anger overwhelmed me. "Toughen up," I would tell myself, my arms tense and my teeth clenched as I walked in the door. Dad would appear, the yelling would start, and the beating would begin.

My mind would race and my adrenaline would be on fire as I fought back. Back in my room I'd cry, beaten physically and mentally and with a feeling of hopelessness consuming me. My self-talk was conflicting. *I want to die. I hate my fucking life! I can't do this anymore. Is it me? Everyone says it is. Maybe I'm the fucked-up one.*

Then the victim child within me would fight back. *Fuck no, it's not me. I did nothing wrong! How could a three-year-old do anything wrong? Fuck everyone.*

I was in high school, but I still felt resentful over having been blamed for causing trouble as a young child. I was exhausted. Each night when it was time to sleep, I couldn't. My thoughts raced as I lay in bed, my body and mind filling with terror.

I don't want the dreams—not tonight. What if tonight is the night my dad shoots me in my sleep? With my parents asleep, I quietly got out of bed and sneaked downstairs to the kitchen. I grabbed a beer and drank it, covering my mouth with my hands so no one would hear me crying. I walked over to the phone and called my girlfriend. "Come pick me up. Let's go out." I climbed out the window and disappeared.

When I was sober, I felt alone, alone with thoughts that frightened and confused me. I was living in hell, and I wanted so badly to kill myself and leave that awful life, but I was too afraid to actually go through with it.

Sitting on the floor in my room, leaning against the wall, I felt an emptiness that I could not explain. I was thinking about my boyfriend, who had cheated on me. He hadn't admitted it, but I knew from the innuendos in his conversations with his friend that it had happened. I was too meek to confront him, and I wasn't even sure how I felt about it. I was trying to put an emotion to my feelings—was I angry, hurt, sad? *Why am I a puppet to everyone around me? What is wrong with me?*

I tried to analyze my thoughts and define my emotions. Inside, my heart was empty. I felt nothing. I stood up and walked into the bathroom, searching the drawers until I found a razor blade. I walked back into my room and took my seat against the wall. *Can I do this?*

I took a deep breath and cut into my wrist, a line about an inch long. It wasn't deep enough to cut my vein, but the pain awakened all my senses. *That felt good.* I cut into the same line a second time, making it deeper, then another line right next to it. I continued to cut across the length of my arm as words formed—slow and steady, ensuring I felt every bit of pain. It hurt, but the pain was euphoric—my head was clear, my mind empty. I felt these words—"I have become comfortably numb"—from the beautiful song by David Gilmour and Roger Waters titled "Comfortably Numb." This song became my anthem.

By the time I was done cutting my arm, I had written "Dave, I love you." It was a message to my boyfriend with words I had not exchanged with him before. It surprised me that I'd written this or thought this. I was bored in our relationship and didn't care if we stayed together. The fact that he'd cheated was my way out—and yet I'd carved these words of love for him into my arm? What was I seeking to gain out of that? *What the fuck is wrong with you?* My thoughts berated me for my actions. Trying to escape my own self-hatred, I left my house, walked into the nearby woods, and smoked a joint.

The attention I got from my friends was shock and awe. My boyfriend, fearing the anger of my father, broke up with me. Embarrassed, I hid my arm so I didn't have to explain it to anyone. My mom's reaction, however, was the one that affected me the most. One morning as she was in the bathroom getting ready for work, she noticed the cuts on my arm. Not knowing anything about drugs except what she got from watching *Miami Vice*, my mom thought the cut marks were from doing heroin. I tried to convince her that I was not a heroin addict, but she didn't believe me. I didn't want to hurt her. It was important for me to have her trust. She was the only adult support I had ever had. I fell to the bathroom floor in front of her and began crying, begging her to believe me that I was not a heroin addict.

When she came home from work that night, I sat her down and explained to her about the drugs I was taking, including their effects and how they made me feel. My mom, never taking so much as a drink, didn't understand, but she listened. I talked to her about drugs throughout the next several years. I thought explaining it to her would make her worry about me less. Whenever I left the house, not knowing when I would return, she would always say the same thing: "Be careful who you get your drugs from." I had no idea at the time how painful that must have been for her, but years later she told me that she worried about me a lot. Praying for my safety each night was how she coped.

One Saturday morning during my senior year in high school, I woke up early and started drinking vodka and orange juice. It was a habit of mine to start drinking early. I was headed downstairs to make another drink when I saw my mom, who was supposed to be at work, lying on the couch. It was odd for her to be lying down since she was usually doing chores of some sort before she headed off to work. I had already made several trips downstairs, so I was pretty drunk when I noticed her. I stumbled up to the couch and noticed her eyes were closed.

"Mom? Mom, are you OK?" She slowly opened her eyes but didn't answer. She was out of it, and I knew something was wrong. She was not completely passed out, but she was so weak she couldn't get up. I sat down beside her and cried, feeling helpless that I didn't know what to do and sorry for myself for being drunk in the first place.

My mom had had a stroke. She spent several weeks in the hospital. I never even went to visit her, so consumed was I with my tortured life. I did quit drinking that day—for the first time—but I continued to do drugs. I was detached from life, an empty shell made emotionless from the drugs I was using.

I wanted to be comfortably numb all the time, and drugs and alcohol helped me feel that way for many years. My grades were failing, and I started cutting classes even more. During my senior year of high school, I cut 85 of the total 180 school days. With a school that size, we had a principal per grade, and our principal would make the rounds, calling all of my friends' houses to find out where my girlfriends and I were hanging out. I had missed so much school that I wasn't going to graduate.

I wanted to graduate since I still had dreams of going to college. When I was in middle school, my oldest sister had taken typing and shorthand classes. I studied her books all the time. Being that my parents owned rental properties and their English was not very good, my siblings and I managed all their books and worked with accountants, lawyers, and the city government for our welfare tenants.

I was smart, and I wanted out. My out was to go to college, but not just any college—Katharine Gibbs College. This was a prestigious secretarial school at the time. Graduates traveled in limousines with the likes of Mike Jagger. I had read about it in a magazine article. I loved music, and I fantasized about getting hired as a secretary and traveling the world with a famous musician—that was my plan out. But in my house, women didn't go to school. We got married and pregnant. That was the old-school thinking of a Sicilian father. But I saw how my mom lived, dependent on my dad for money and being told what to do and how to live her life. I wanted no part of that. *I am never going to be dependent on a man!*

I continued studying my sister's books and took the same classes she'd taken in high school. By my senior year I had mastered 85 words a minute on a manual typewriter. I practiced stenography by typing as I watched the news. I could keep up, writing 140 words per minute. I was good at it. While I failed most of my other classes, my typing teacher recommended me to Katharine Gibbs College, and I was accepted, including a two-year, half-tuition scholarship.

The only thing holding me back was my dad—he wouldn't let me go since it was in another city, and I couldn't get financial aid to pay for the remaining cost. My parents made too much money for me to be eligible for any more financial aid, and he wouldn't pay the rest. The counselors at school were useless since they told me I needed to make amends with my dad to somehow get him to pay for the remainder. I knew that wasn't going to happen, so I gave up on my dream.

My principal talked to all the kids who were not going to graduate, and I was one of them. He told me if I agreed to go to summer school to take several courses that I was failing, he'd let me go to graduation day with the rest of my classmates. I wanted to go since all my friends would be there—and also because I hadn't told my family yet that I needed to go to summer school to earn my degree.

On graduation day, as I waited in line, I pulled my usual antics and bullied one of the popular girls, a girl I'd had an ongoing feud with, calling her slut, whore, and other mean things. When they called my name, I walked up and received my graduation booklet, only it was empty inside. I was told afterward that once I completed summer school the school would give me my certificate.

My parents attended my graduation, and when I got home, my family—aunts and uncles and grandparents—were all there to celebrate. After I revealed to my parents why I had no certificate, my family laid into me about the usual stuff—the drugs I was doing, the friends I hung out with, and the fact that I hadn't actually graduated that day. I started drinking again at what was supposed to be my graduation celebration; then I took off in anger when a fight with my dad ensued. That day was no different than any other.

I did make it to summer school, however, along with my best friend and my brother and his friend, who were both in the ninth grade. Each day we'd drive in together after a night of drinking and partying in New York City. We'd come straight home from the bars, stop for breakfast, and then go by a 7-Eleven to pick up NoDoz so we could make it through class. I finished my classes that summer and finally earned my graduation certificate, but it wasn't until several years later that I went back to the school to pick it up.

I didn't know where to go from there. I continued to do drugs on a regular basis. All my friends were doing drugs, so I didn't stand out. Many of them were more extreme in their drug use than I was and eventually had less fortunate endings than mine. I'm not sure if the drugs were an escape for them like it was for me or if they were just having fun. As some of my friends went off to college, I stayed behind, stuck in my version of hell.

I was working as a secretary in a local factory, but I was starting to feel like my life was turning out like my mom's. I talked with my mom and grandmother about college, and they offered to speak to my dad about my going to the local community college.

After a lot of pressure from my mom and grandmother, my dad offered to pay for the local community college on the condition that I stop doing drugs and partying with my friends. But it wasn't my dream. I dropped out after only two semesters and continued my destructive behaviors.

When I think back, I know that this was a choice I made based on the victim curse that I'd placed on myself. I could have continued my studies in a local school, but I chose not to so that I could remain a victim of my dad and his abuse. I had a victim card, and I continued to play that card well.

For two years after graduation, I continued to live at my parents' house. When I was twenty, I finally moved out. I had talked to my mom about it, and while she didn't want me to leave, she understood. The only thing she said was that I needed to tell my dad myself. I knew if I didn't, I would never be allowed back in the house again. I wanted to be able to come back to see my mom, so I made a plan of how I would break the news.

I packed up my car with my belongings and waited for him to return home from work. As I sat in the driver's seat with my car running, I was nervous. My hands were sweating, holding tightly onto the steering wheel. I saw my dad pull into the driveway and get out of his truck. I called him over to my car, rolled down the window and told him I was moving out. Immediately he started screaming and yelling at me as I had expected, but I didn't hear what he said. I put the car in reverse and drove off.

At the time, I was dating someone I had been friends with in high school, and he was looking for an apartment. It wasn't a healthy relationship for me. This guy had cheated on me twice already, and I had violent thoughts of taking one of my dad's guns and killing him and his other girlfriends as revenge. But I was young. *He's not horrible to me,* I convinced myself. So I told him I'd move in with him. I wanted to get out of my house, and this was a convenient way for me to escape.

After a year, my dad said my boyfriend and I needed to get married since it looked bad for the family that I was living in sin. He even offered to pay for the wedding. Young and stupid and with my boyfriend having student loans to pay, I asked this boy to marry me. We were both from Italian families, and Italians are known for giving *la busta,* "the envelope," as a gift. In other words, if we got married, we could expect envelopes of money.

Six months later we were married and received $12,000 in gifts. Everyone had given us *la busta*—except my brother, who gave us an 8 ball (eighth of an ounce) of cocaine to celebrate the occasion.

I was twenty-two when I married my first husband, and I followed two traditions the day of my wedding. The first was that I let my father walk me down the aisle. I debated it long and hard. I didn't want him walking me down the aisle, but ultimately I caved since he was the one paying for the wedding. The second was the father-daughter wedding dance. When I was young and my father was drunk and would dance, if he was in a good mood I'd try to dance with him. He would swing me around almost violently as I tried to hold on.

I was nervous about dancing with him the night of my wedding, but it was a slow dance, so how bad could it get? During that dance, my dad, already drunk, proceeded to tell me that the reason he drank and was an alcoholic was because of me. With two hundred people watching, there was nothing I could do or say without creating a scene.

So, angry, hurt, and confused—the way he'd made me feel for literally as long as I could remember—I sucked it up. I never said a word, and I finished out our dance.

While taking college classes a few years later, I took a class on poetry. One of the poems I was assigned to read was "My Papa's Waltz" by Theodore Roethke. The poem was chilling in its similarity to my experiences with my father. In the poem, the young boy recalls dancing with his father, becoming almost woozy from the alcohol on his father's breath. The dance was violent and ungraceful, with the boy clinging to his father and his father's heavy steps knocking pans from their shelves and causing the boy's mother to look on with disapproval. The father kept the beat by patting the boy's head, but the pats were hard thumps. The supposedly innocent and loving act of dancing with a parent was instead a painfully awkward interaction fraught with a desire to be loved countered by overwhelming fear.

I wrote an analysis of this poem for my class. To me, the description of the father reeked of the abuse and alcoholism I was so familiar with in my own father. I remember finishing my paper with this line: "Because I too am that little girl who has danced this waltz with my father."

When I returned from my honeymoon, I found out that my father had been caught having an affair and that my mom finally had summoned the nerve to take action. I knew it wasn't the first time he'd had an affair since I had overheard him talking on the phone about such things in the past. In fact, he had boasted about being with other women all the time. He would laugh wryly as if it were only a joke, but I knew the truth.

He once came home with an affliction of crabs and told my mom it was from old sheets in a hotel room. Whether she bought it or not at the time didn't matter—she had her young children to care for and she needed him. But this time, her children were grown, and she had proof of this affair.

Strong as she was, my mom froze all their bank accounts and filed for divorce. My dad moved in with his girlfriend. Rosetta was married and had moved out by that time, my brother had joined the army, and I was newly married. My mom and Princess were alone in that house. My dad could show up at any moment, making their life at home constantly unpredictable. They were never able to feel at ease or safe. I visited as often as I could along with my sister and brother, but those visits would turn into arguments whenever my dad showed up, which he did often. He wanted my mom to take him back, but she refused. I was scared for her but also proud of her.

During those months, my father became even more violent, fighting with all of his kids and blaming my mother for all his troubles. That Christmas we were all celebrating, and he came in angry as hell. He threw a handful of Christmas cards into the living room and started yelling at us about how we'd abandoned him and sided with our mother.

I started after him, yelling that he was the one who'd made the choice to have an affair. I lunged at him, and thankfully my brother grabbed me and held on so I couldn't get to my father even as I struggled to break free.

That episode ended with my brother and father in our garage, my brother holding a tire iron and threatening to kill him if he didn't leave. My dad was drunk and my brother, older now and stronger, intimidated him. My dad left.

Over the next year, my dad threatened to kill my mom and sister several times. One day in his fit of anger he tried to do just that by throwing a frying pan at my mother's head. It barely missed her. She ran to a neighbor's house, and when the police came, she was able to file a restraining order.

This low point for my dad was my out. I reached out to him and said I wanted to speak to him about the divorce. I played super nice and acted like I felt bad for him. Then I asked to borrow $2,000 from him. It was a scam, and as I took his money, I left knowing I would no longer speak to him.

In fact, it would be eighteen years before I saw him again. Still, in those years I had fights with him in my head, yelling at him out loud while driving alone in my car or cursing him as I continued to sleep only under the safety of my covers, blankets over my head so I could feel protected against the world. I was still angry. I hated him and what he had done to me. Even though he was no longer in my life, I still couldn't escape his grasp.

Shortly after my marriage, I moved to the Bronx with my husband. We lived in an apartment near a Jewish temple. One early Saturday morning as I walked out into the street, I noticed there was a street fair going on. It was a Jewish holiday, and vendors had set up stands selling foods and goods. There were at least a hundred people already out walking the street.

We had no off-street parking with our apartment, so I had to park on the street. I found my car that morning, got in, and pulled out into the street. Immediately, a driver in a car behind me honked to let me know I'd apparently cut him off. In response, I did what came naturally to me—I flipped him the bird. Midway down the street, one of the riders of the car behind me threw a soda can out the window and hit my car. I stopped and got out.

There were two boys in the car. I yelled, "Why the fuck are you throwing shit at my car?"

The driver got out of the car. "You cut us off when you pulled out!"

I cursed back, and midsentence the driver of the car reached into his car and grabbed a Big Gulp, one of those extra-large drinks in plastic cups you could buy at 7-Eleven. He flung it right at me. It hit me in the face, knocking my glasses off. I was covered in soda.

My anger instantly intensified. My arms tensed up, and I jumped the guy. I knocked him to the ground and started punching him. His friend had jumped out of the car and now grabbed me by my hair and threw me to the ground. Both of them started punching me as I tried to fight them off.

I lay there defeated as they hurried to their car and drove off. I pulled myself together and stood up. Everyone on the street from the fair was watching me, but no one said a word.

"You're all going to burn in hell," I said to the crowd staring at me. "Every fucking one of you. Fuck you! I hope you all fucking burn in hell!"

I got into my car and drove down the street about two blocks until I came to a stop sign. My entire body was shaking. My heart was racing. *Fuck, fuck, fuck!* I slammed my hands against the steering wheel and began to cry. I was there a while until I heard another car honk. I looked up in the mirror, and it was those same boys. They were laughing and yelling at me.

I took off and drove around the neighborhood while they followed me. I made it to the gas station down the street and parked my car. I ran as fast as I could, trying to make it inside the gas station, but they caught up to me before I could get there. Suddenly I felt a pull on my shirt, and down I went. One of the boys was on me, punching me in the chest and face, while the other one kicked me from the side. I tried to fight them off, but I was powerless. When the gas station attendant saw what was happening, he came running out and ran them off.

The attendant called the police, and when they came I explained what happened. I called my husband, who came to the gas station on his bicycle. After I described the car and the two boys to the police, my husband took off on his bike and the police left in their car to search for the boys. They soon found them.

When the police came back, they told me that the kids were part of a family that "owned" the neighborhood. "They know who you are now," they said, "and there's nothing we can do about it." Their advice was for us to move.

Two weeks later we moved to the suburbs in Westchester. I had a few black and blues from the fight, but that day the biggest bruise I had was on my ego. I knew I couldn't continue fighting like that. My rage had come on so quickly, just like my dad's. It scared me, but I didn't know how to stop it. *Once my dad dies, this anger will go away*, I told myself. That was my last fistfight, but my anger continued.

Just like I had adopted my dad's rage, I also had become a functioning abuser like he was. I was working a full-time job and had also started a business on the side typing résumés for friends and transcribing Dictaphone-recorded spoken notes from the doctors in the hospital where I worked. I had also purchased a computer and began teaching myself programming.

I had a fire in me to be successful. I absorbed myself in my work, and yet I still looked for the escape. I drank heavily and went to work hungover or while still tripping after a weekend of hallucinogens. I worked hard and held onto jobs, but I played just as hard.

Being in my own skin was still so painful. On the outside I was confident, smart, and successful. On the inside I was a little girl, pained by the abuse of her father and abandoned by God to fend for herself. I was judgmental of myself and of others. I saw life as a glass completely empty. There was so much negativity in the world to begin with, and I only saw the bad. I put up a good front, but inside I wanted out. I wanted nothing to do with life. I saw myself as a proud victim, torn between having the strength to have survived my childhood on the one hand and yet still paying the price with my eternal suffering on the other.

While I wanted permanence in being comfortably numb, that pursuit was catching up to me. At twenty-five I was given the opportunity to go back to college when my company offered 100 percent tuition reimbursement. I signed up immediately and found I really enjoyed school this time. I was going to college at night, taking accounting and computer programming classes and maintaining a 3.7 GPA while working ninety-hour workweeks. I was driven by my work and school. It gave me a high and a confidence I hadn't felt before, yet I was burned out. I wanted so badly to be successful, and the drugs were getting in the way. It was then that I decided that drugs were no longer for me. I quit marijuana first, then a few years later all the rest, and I was clean by the time I was twenty-seven.

I wasn't done with alcohol though. When you are raised with an alcoholic, you risk becoming an alcoholic yourself. My siblings all have a different relationship with alcohol. My oldest sister only drinks on occasion, and one glass would make her drunk with giggles. My other sister never drank until she was well into her thirties, and I've only seen her have a glass of wine once or twice since she abstains for the most part. My brother has had his share of ups and downs with it over his lifetime.

I put myself in the category of alcoholic as my motto was always this: "Everything I do, I do in excess." Whether it was working, drinking, smoking, or doing drugs, I enjoyed doing it to the extreme. I hadn't had a drink for five years after the incident with my mom's stroke when I started drinking again. This time it didn't take over my life like it had in high school. I only drank occasionally, once every few months, and even then, it was just a couple of drinks. I finally had alcohol under control.

Escape for me in my earlier years always meant drugs and alcohol. My brother always jokes that those early years were six years of time that I can't remember. It was more than ten years, in all honesty. Drugs and alcohol kept me numb through my darkest times and allowed me to maneuver through the world without those around me ever knowing that my mind harbored dark secrets that resulted in anger issues, in uncontrollable dark thoughts toward those around me, including myself, and in a deep-seated unhappiness that kept me from enjoying the present moments.

I tried to erase my pain with drugs, but that only masked the deeper wounds I hid inside. And while I was able to get sober, the damage that had been done to me as a child remained. I was a victim at the hands of my father and still feeling alone with a pain in my heart—I had carried this with me into my adulthood. I was angry and resentful, but I convinced myself that it was good for me since it meant that I was a survivor, that I was tough.

At least I thought I was tough. Many years ago, when I was in my thirties, I was watching the movie *Divine Secrets of the Ya-Ya Sisterhood* with my niece, one of Rosetta's daughters, who was in her late teens. There's a scene where Ashley Judd's character has a nervous breakdown, and she starts beating her kids with a belt. My dad didn't have a nervous breakdown—he turned to anger in a split second on a regular basis. Still, while watching that scene, I started crying. Not a few tears rolling down my face but a hard cry, one of those where you start hyperventilating because you can't breathe, and you're literally bent over, hysterical, like you were just told someone close to you died.

I couldn't stop, and I ran out of the room into the bathroom until I could calm down. When I finally came out again, I apologized to my niece. "I don't know what happened," I said to her. "I did not expect that."

And she responded so sweetly and innocently. "It's OK," she said. "Mommy told me that Grandpa used to hit you." Her voice was so soothing, as if I had the support of my oldest sister with me even though she was two thousand miles away, and it made it all OK.

THE CLINIC WAS IN a nondescript, ordinary-looking building, but you knew what was happening inside by those who were picketing outside, taunting and yelling, "Baby killer!" They were judging all the scared young girls walking into the building—and I was one of them. *I'm a monster.* Torn between raising a child while still doing a lot of drugs or aborting the child within me, I convinced myself I was doing the right thing.

The first time I was pregnant, I was twenty years old. I had recently moved in with my boyfriend, before he became my husband. I was doing a lot of drugs and making just above minimum wage and was not ready for a child. I couldn't go to my family, so I turned to my boyfriend's parents. After much discussion, my boyfriend and I decided to abort the child I was carrying. I was depressed and sad about the decision, but I felt it was the right choice for me.

My boyfriend didn't come with me since he had to work that day. I was mad at him for choosing to work, but he thought he might lose his job if he took the day off, so I conceded. I didn't go alone. I took with me someone I could count on, my sister the Princess. She, of all people, I didn't think would understand, but I was afraid to turn to anyone else. My sister was a year older than me in school and straight and narrow. She didn't drink or do drugs, and she obeyed my father. Throughout high school she'd berated me, called me whore and slut and told people we were not related. But since my siblings always come through, she rescued me, protecting me from my father, who would certainly have killed me if he had found out. She took me to the clinic and watched over me that night.

And just like that I was no longer pregnant. I thought, *That was a close call.* And immediately I went on birth control. I was not going to have kids. My girlfriends and I talked about being pregnant and harboring "alien spawn." The thought of having something grow inside me was freaky and unnatural. Hearing kids scream in a restaurant or airplane made my arms tense up and the blood rush through my veins, that same feeling I had walking into my parent's house. *Never.*

A few years later, I took a job in a children's hospital in Valhalla, New York. I loved that job. I was a stenographer and secretary for the psychiatry department, and I spent a lot of time with the kids. Many were fighting serious illnesses, some terminal, and it pained me to see that kids could be healthy one day then so sick the next. Just out of the blue, their life changed so drastically.

The worry and pain in the parents' faces was apparent—it was the same pain and worry I had seen in my mom as she tried to protect us kids from the awful man she had married. I saw the worry my mom had put on herself and the trouble we had given her on top of it all. My mom was consumed with worry, and her life was not her own—it belonged to my father, and her kids consumed her. And it was the same worry and pain I felt whenever I saw my brother sick from his asthma.

Growing up in an abusive house had made me a control freak. I had earned the right to make my own rules and control all my circumstances, mostly to protect my emotions, and having kids meant you had no control. I was afraid to be vulnerable—I couldn't be because not being vulnerable was all I knew in terms of how to survive. I left my job at the hospital after two years because the kids' stories made me go home at night and cry. *Definitely not having kids.*

Little girls have dreams of weddings, the number of kids they'll bear, and what their husbands will be like. I never wanted to be married, having witnessed my parents' marriage. My mom was dependent on my dad as the main provider of for their kids, and she needed him. I wasn't going to fall into that trap. My dreams were not of marriage but of having kids. Kids from foster care, kids who were lost and damaged like I was, kids with whom I could connect, love, protect, and fix. I would be their savior. I thought when I was older and ready, I would adopt two older kids, boys or girls, and take them in to love and support the way kids should be loved. But I wasn't ready. I was still angry, and I was afraid of turning into my father and hurting those same kids I wanted to adopt and protect.

Most of us go through life blindly following someone else's plan, and that's what I did. I married very young since that's what people did in those days. You got married, and so with a lot of pressure from my family, I did too. Only the pressure didn't stop once you got married because the next thing everyone wanted was a baby.

Some of our friends were having kids at the time, and when they came over to hang out, I became the caretaker of those babies—not because their parents weren't good parents but because I enjoyed changing diapers and watching the kids. That's when I caught baby fever. After talking about it with my husband, we decided to stop birth control and start having kids. I was sober, and I thought if I had kids then I would be able to handle being a parent.

If only it were that easy. I had expected to get pregnant right away, but the months went by, and no pregnancy occurred. Eventually the months turned into years. When I wanted to get pregnant, I couldn't. I blamed myself. *Is this punishment for the abortion I had? What did I do wrong to deserve this?* My mantra returned: *Why me?*

And I was a victim once again.

I felt alone with no one to turn to. Sure, I was married, but I wasn't happy in my marriage. My priorities in life were working and school. My husband's priorities were working and getting high. We had some common ground with playing video games, but we were growing apart fast and fighting about it a lot.

I wanted him to change. I wanted him to stop getting high and be sober like me. He was still experimenting with drugs and sex and didn't want to grow up or change for me. He was a flirt with other women. I was extremely jealous, but he was charismatic, and I always succumbed to his apologies. I was enabling him in our marriage. I was aware of it, but I allowed it because in return I got to keep my independence. *At least he doesn't hit me*, I told myself, but I couldn't help but want more. *Always alone, even in marriage.*

My victim-self wanted to escape. I needed to survive. I didn't care what my husband thought; I cared only about what I wanted. I wanted to move to California where all the cool tech jobs were, but my husband wanted to stay in New York with his family. I was itching for a change. I needed something different, new. I was suffocating in my own skin. I was looking outward for love and acceptance instead of within myself. My husband wasn't giving me that, and I wanted to move on.

After ten years of marriage, I asked my husband for a divorce, and we decided to part ways. Our separation lasted about a month before my husband had a change of heart and said he wanted to come with me. I agreed on the condition that he stop doing drugs and "grow up," especially when it came to other women.

We made it as far as Las Vegas, where my brother was living. My company let me keep my job working remotely. Once we got there, it was as if nothing had happened, and we continued to work on having kids. It was probably not the best idea considering the state of our marriage, but my husband was showing signs of change, and I was comfortable enough with the escape I had just made by leaving my hometown.

Going to a fertility clinic was the next step. We couldn't afford in vitro, a fairly new procedure at the time that our insurance didn't cover. We wanted to find out what the cause was—why there was no pregnancy. So ensued five invasive surgical tests, some under full anesthesia, some local—all painful, both physically and emotionally—to determine the cause, but we still had no diagnosis.

Reading everything I could about how to get pregnant, I joined an online infertility support group and bought every book on the female body and what it took to get pregnant. I charted my menstrual cycle. Every day was filled with taking waking temperatures and examining my vagina and anything that oozed out of it. Having lots of sex, spending hours with legs up against the headboard "to make it stick," and so on—you name it, I tried it. And every month was worse than the one before it. I'd get my period and then take a pregnancy test anyway. *Maybe this time,* I thought. *My sister had three kids, and I vaguely remember her saying she had vaginal bleeding the first few weeks in the beginning.* I tried to convince myself.

That big minus on the pregnancy stick that tore at my heart grew more devastating to handle every month. I'd lie in bed after each negative result, crying at another lost opportunity to have a child, feeling sorry for myself. *Why me?*

By my early thirties, this had become my personal mantra. *Why me? Why do I continue to be victimized? What have I done in this world to deserve all this negativity in my life? Life is unfair to me. Will I ever find happiness and feel joy in the everyday aspects of life?*

My walls grew higher, as my heart broke in pieces behind it. Two pregnancies—hope!—then two miscarriages. *That's three strikes now. I don't deserve this. I don't deserve to suffer like this. Why me?* It had been five years of no birth control, just winging it—and almost five more years in clinics getting tests to see what was "wrong with us" and trying to get pregnant. For ten years of our lives, we were consumed with trying to have kids.

Then it happened—I was pregnant again. By this time I was thirty-six years old, and because of my age and how long it had taken to get pregnant, it was considered a high-risk pregnancy.

The pregnancy was difficult, but not in a physical way. I was fine, and being pregnant suited me. I was healthy and carrying well. I had cravings for fried chicken, and strawberries made me sick. *No alien spawn in here—this is great!* My heart was glowing, and it showed on the outside. I'd be lying if I said emotionally it was that easy though. I worried every day that I might lose this child in my belly. A child whose future I had already started dreaming about, just like I had before the two previous miscarriages.

My daydreams were of me playing with my child—he or she would come running across the room, arms outstretched, running to his or her mom, and that mom was me. I replayed that vision dozens of time in my head. I wanted so badly to feel loved. I was yearning for love, the love I'd never had from my dad as a child. These visions were how I thought I could fill the huge hole in my heart. *With a child I won't feel so alone, so empty. I'll have purpose.* I was a control freak, and it sucked to be so out of control while waiting for this dream to become a reality.

We got to see the baby early on with technologies that a normal gynecology office didn't have at the time. At first, we had two babies, but eventually there was a "vanishing twin," which was common with the fertility drug Clomid that I'd taken. We had been told in advance about this, and while we were excited to have twins at first, we were also not surprised when we lost one of the babies. We nicknamed the remaining baby Spot because on the first sonogram picture he was just a tiny speck. Then Spot grew to be called Big Spot.

At five months pregnant, I was working and making decent money, but my husband was starting a new business and had no income. I wanted to be financially stable before we had a kid, but I'd learned early on that you had no control over your life when it came to kids. *We'll make it through somehow.*

When the twin towers collapsed the morning of September 11, 2001, my negative view of the world once again came crashing down on me. I sat and stared wide-eyed at the television in shock, crying for myself and crying for my unborn child. The world was at war, and conspiracy theories abounded. I was sad and stressed out. I felt scared for me and my child. I was Linda Hamilton in *The Terminator* when she was pregnant during the apocalypse.

Also that very day, my husband had a kickoff meeting scheduled for his new business venture. Due to the attack, however, few people attended the meeting. My husband hadn't taken a salary in almost a year, and now his new business would never have a chance to take off.

And this was how the remainder of my pregnancy continued. I thought between 9/11 and my husband's financial setbacks, the worst that could happen had already happened, but I was wrong.

I couldn't wait for the next ultrasound to see Big Spot. I was worried since at the last appointment we had been due to find out the sex of the baby, but the doctors hadn't been able to tell. It was odd at five months to not know the sex of the baby, but our doctor assured us that we'd find out at the next appointment. I felt like I was having a boy, and I was excited to get that confirmation. It would be the same boy I had lost at the age of twenty. *He came back. It's time.* I wanted him to come back. I realized then that I still hadn't gotten over the first boy I'd chosen to abort, and I wanted so badly for this pregnancy to "make it right." But I left the doctor's office that day disappointed and frustrated again without any answers.

At our next appointment our doctor told us some surprising news. "The baby's sex is ambiguous," he said, "and there could be problems."

What the hell does that mean?

The doctor recommended a second opinion, which gave us the same news: "It's most likely a boy, but we can't be sure."

I wish these doctors wouldn't think out loud like they do. They really have no compassion or consideration for your feelings.

The sonogram test revealed that while the doctors could see testicles, there was no visual penis. They scheduled a more advanced sonogram, one that is very common today but was rare at the time. After taking a 3-D image of my baby's genitals to see what its gender was, the outcome was the same.

Testicles and no penis.

We were assigned a counselor and gender specialist. What they told us next was the most unusual and shocking news you could imagine:

"Don't tell people the gender of the baby."

"Your baby may be a hermaphrodite."

"Name the baby a non-gender-specific name."

"By the age of three you will have to select a gender for your baby and have sex-reassignment surgery."

What the fuck? What were we supposed to do with that information?

When someone is so obviously pregnant, the two things people ask are "When are you due?" and "What are you having?"

How the fuck am I not going to tell people the gender of the baby?

Every time I was asked the gender, I calmly responded, "We're not going to find out until the baby comes." Then I would find a hiding spot and cry until I couldn't cry any longer. *I wish my baby had cancer or a heart problem,* I thought. Not that I really wished that, but it would be easier to tell people that our baby had cancer than to tell them it might be a hermaphrodite. *This was taboo!* No one talked about this, even in the year 2001.

We changed his nickname to Ambiguously Gay Spot and tried to make light of it, but it was a painful time. We went every month for counseling visits and follow-up sonograms, hoping for good news. *Maybe this time we will see something.* Every day was a blur by this time.

Gender-neutral nursery, gender-neutral names, hiding our secret—and these were supposed to be months of excitement and anticipation. I had been taking Bradley Method childbirth classes since I had planned on having a home birth in my bathtub, but this could no longer be an option. I was high-risk and needed to be in the hospital when the baby was born. The doctors would need to "inspect" this child that I was carrying the minute he was born. No scheduled circumcision for him (or her) in the hospital, and everyone was ordered to *not touch this baby* when "it" came out.

Without going into the labor, delivery, and C-section details, when my baby finally arrived, the specialists came in to inspect it. My child was definitely a boy! He had a penis—it was all there, just hiding under some skin that was pulling it down and inside so it couldn't be seen. It was beyond great news. He was a healthy baby boy—testicles, penis, and all. We later found out that this complication was due to a common condition caused by, once again, the fertility drug Clomid. I vaguely remembered reading something about it. *I'm relieved, but I wonder how many parents don't receive the same news?*

About a year after having our firstborn, we tried for another child. My husband didn't want to go through it again, but I really wanted a sibling for our son. We never talked about how he felt, and I never thought about what he was going through. I was selfish in thinking he wasn't hurting emotionally as much as I was. I only wanted what I thought was best for me. After much convincing, we were back to the clinic, trying for baby number two.

I immediately got pregnant this time, but about two and a half months in, I miscarried. Then another pregnancy and another miscarriage, this time at three and a half months. Each miscarriage was devastating to me. My heart ached from the emptiness I felt and the feeling that it was my fault "for being the bad kid." I'd cry for days and weeks on end. I was depressed, but I hid it well. No one ever wants to talk about the bad things that go on in a life. I was going through the motions of life during the day, and when I had moments to myself, I'd cry and think, *What did I do wrong to deserve this? Why me?* My mantra continued. I was still the victim. *It's not fair.*

Eventually I got pregnant a third time. *Third time's a charm again, right?* By four and half months along, I was wearing maternity clothes and excited to be on that crazy adventure. Two of my good friends, at least ten years younger than I was, were also pregnant, and we were all due within weeks of one another. We talked about our babies and how they would grow up together. It was the first child for both of them, so there was a lot of excitement with all of our news. While I was cautious due to my previous miscarriages, once I hit the four-month mark, I was more at ease with having this baby.

The baby had been growing well from the start, but then we discovered during a routine visit that the growing had stopped. The doctors wanted me to take an amniocentesis test in which they put a very long needle into my belly and sucked out amniotic fluid from my baby's sac to test it for birth defects. This test was a risk in itself, and I'd always sworn I would never do the test if it ever came down to it. The doctors were able to convince me to take the test. The results were pure excruciating, emotional pain. Our baby had Trisomy 18. Trisomy 18 is a chromosome defect in which every cell in the baby's body is defective. This is what they told us this time:

"The baby may not live past seven months."

"You will need to give birth to a stillborn."

"If the baby lives through the pregnancy, it will most likely die within a few hours."

"Best-case scenario, it would die in a few days."

When the doctors tell you this news, you basically have two options—continue with the pregnancy or have a second-trimester abortion, which apparently is legal if you have a baby with this type of condition.

I can't do it. I can't bury a child. I can't go through with what lies ahead. I'm too weak. I'm broken. I will fall apart.

I badly wanted to carry the baby until he died and then bury him, but I wasn't strong enough.

We chose abortion, which led to two more options. We could go to the local clinic and have it done or fly to California, where they specialized in these types of situations. For financial reasons, we chose the local clinic, and this time my husband came with me. He waited in the front room while I was examined. The baby was only showing the size of a thirteen-week-old baby, but I was almost five months along at this point.

I cried in the office when they asked me if I was sure I wanted this. Through my tears I said, "No, I don't want this!" They sent a team of people to come in and counsel me. They didn't know the reason I was having to abort the baby. Someone said I looked like I was twenty-two and so young and asked if I'd considered putting the baby up for adoption instead. Still crying, I was able to explain my situation to them—I was thirty-nine and my baby was not going to live. They understood, and they walked me into the operating room. And under anesthesia I went.

It didn't matter what choice I made, I would have broken apart anyway. I refused to move on, and I didn't care what people thought. I skipped my friends' baby showers and birthday

parties—any occasion, for that matter. I couldn't be around pregnant people. I couldn't be around people. I was alone, depressed,
and thinking about suicide again. I needed help. I started seeing
a therapist, alone. If my then-husband felt bad about it, I barely
knew, so consumed was I with my own grieving. We rarely talked
about it together. I was unaware of how he coped with our losses
since when we talked about it, our discussions were superficial.

And no one else wanted to talk about it. This was another
taboo subject. People said dumb things like "At least you got
pregnant again" and "You'll get over it—it just takes time." Their
responses were fake, and according to my therapist, were only
meant to help themselves feel better, not me. If only they knew I
still wasn't over my first abortion at twenty. They'd never understand that either. Each abortion, each miscarriage, was not just
a pregnancy. Each one was a child, my child, a child that had a
future with first steps, school plays, and graduations. Each child
was a lifetime of me being a mom.

My therapist put me on antidepressants, and I went to therapy a few times a week. I learned three things about myself
while in therapy:

First, I was really broken, but I wasn't ready to be fixed. I
thought I was doing a great job talking about my depression,
sadness, and suicidal thoughts. To my surprise, however, my
therapist told me that in the thirty-plus years she had been in her
occupation, I was the hardest person to open up that she had ever
met. "You have built a wall around you," she said, "so thick I
can't get through to you."

Second, I really cared about my siblings. My therapist asked
me to tell her about my siblings. A big smile came across my face.
She asked me why bringing them up brought me so much joy,

and I replied, "We're all so unique in our own ways, but we are always there for one another when it counts. I love my siblings."

Third, I had a lot of guilt over my decision to abort my last child. Boy, was that an emotional session. My therapist thought it would be a good idea to do a role-playing session regarding my last abortion. She played my unborn child, whose life I had recently decided to end. She asked me to speak to her as if she were my child. "I'm so sorry. I'm sorry I killed you. I'm so sorry. I love you."

I cried hysterically, apologizing to my child for abandoning him. I harbored so much anger and hatred for myself, so much guilt. My therapist allowed me to hug my imaginary baby and get forgiveness from him, to release my guilt over what I had done. I went through the motions, but it didn't make me feel any better about myself.

After just a few months, I wanted off the antidepressants. I felt like I was forcing myself to talk in therapy and decided this was no longer for me. I was "fixed" enough to go about it on my own and start interacting with the world again.

The first time I decided to attend an occasion with friends and people was a funeral. Unfortunately, one of my friends who was pregnant had a younger brother who was killed in a car accident at only seventeen. I went to the memorial service and grieved not only for him but also selfishly for my son. This young boy's funeral was also my way of saying goodbye to my son.

I spoke to my girlfriend, and the compassion she had for me on a day when she was grieving herself showed such strength. I spoke with her and her mom a lot in the months afterward, and in our conversations we grieved together. I didn't have to hide from them, and I didn't want to avoid their grief as others did mine. I always asked about her and her brother, calling him by his name and asking her personal questions like "How are you feeling when you walk into his room?" and "What are you doing with his belongings?" My friend had made a beautiful quilt from his clothing, and I asked her about each of the shirts and what it reminded her of. In return, she would ask me about the nursery we had set up and if my milk was coming in.

She always asked me about how I was doing—I mean, *really* asked me how I was doing—and I talked to her about things I couldn't say to other people. I could tell her how I would sit in the nursery and cry for my unborn child, and I knew she understood my grief. We understood each other—our topics not taboo, our responses not fake.

When I thought I was well enough, I started thinking about having another child. Only this time I realized that I had become so consumed with having a biological child that I had forgotten about my dreams of adopting. I had wanted to adopt since I was young—that was my original dream of being a parent, so why not now? I wanted to be a parent, and I didn't care if I got pregnant to do it. After much discussion, the decision was made, and off to an adoption agency we went. After five months of tests, finger-printing, interviews, and home visits, we were finally approved.

Just know that I think about you every day and my heart aches until your arrival. I know it sounds far-fetched, but when you have your children someday, you will understand the love and hurt that are blurred when you love your children so much, even before they arrive.

I wrote this in a journal for my future child, and while I was patient, hopeful, and very excited, my heart ached. I wanted another child so badly, a sibling for my son who had just turned two. I sat in the nursery for hours on end, just staring and rocking and sometimes crying. Then another blow came when I was laid off from my job. My husband's business hadn't taken off, and so my income had been paying for most of our expenses.

We had to live off of my severance pay, and in the meantime I went back to school to pick up some additional computer certifications. Things were not very stable when we received a call that a baby boy had been born and we had been selected as the adopting parents. We talked about it, but the timing just wasn't right. We couldn't accept our child. I was devastated when we had to put our plans on hold.

C'mon, God, seriously? Why do you keep doing this to me? WTF did I do wrong? Why me? I still didn't believe in God, but I had to blame someone for my troubles. I cried for three days in that chair in the nursery.

Several months went by, and I was back at work. My company had rehired me in another division. This job, however, required me to travel extensively, teaching technical classes in different cities. Each session was five days long. I would leave Sunday afternoons and return Friday evenings, with only one day off in between for three weeks in a row at a time. After my three weeks, then I would have two weeks off.

I didn't like the idea of traveling, but I thought the two weeks of uninterrupted time at home would be quality time I could spend with my son. And by that time I had my mom's help too. When I took the job, my mom had agreed to move from New York to Las Vegas so she could help me while I worked. She had done that for my sister for many years. My nieces were older now, and my sister didn't need my mom's help any longer.

Then the agency called with another situation: two little girls, sisters, one three years old and one sixteen months old. I was ready. I wanted a girl badly, and two was a blessing! Only this scenario wasn't right for us either. I was gone a lot, and it would be hard for my husband to bear all the work of raising three kids, even with my mom's help. *Damn, will this ever happen? WTF?*

As much as I wanted those girls to be my daughters, we just couldn't say yes. Or at least my husband couldn't. I carried around more anger and resentment because I'd wanted to bring those girls home. I blamed my husband, who I thought was selfish and lazy.

No one cares about me. No one has my interests at heart. I hate everyone. Life sucks.

I went through the motions of work and taking care of my family when I was home, but I could feel myself slipping away from them emotionally. I lost patience with my son since he was used to having Dad and Grandma take care of him instead of me. I didn't know how he liked his sandwiches or what TV shows he watched. Instead of learning how to interact with him, I retreated to my room and sulked in my own pity.

About a month later, I woke up frantic. I'd had a dream that we received a call for a blond-haired newborn baby boy that left me with an intense need to get ready in case it wasn't just a dream. *Where is the baby-name list? Do I have everything I need to bring home a baby? Is the nursery ready?* I was running around in a panic. The feeling was strong, and I knew he was coming. My mom called shortly afterward. When she asked me what I was doing, I told her I was looking for the baby-names list, and she freaked. She'd had a similar dream. *OMG, this is really happening!*

And it did. Within a couple of days we received a call from the agency that a baby boy had been born and we were the selected parents. In that moment I understood what it must be like for a man to find out his wife was ready to give birth. I freaked out and started jumping up and down. My mom was there, and we both were jumping and hugging and screaming with excitement. My son caught the excitement and called out, "The baby's coming; the baby's coming!"

Suddenly I yelled, "I'm going to puke!" I started gagging and hyperventilating and had to run outside to get fresh air. My mom was laughing, telling me to calm down, but I was so excited that I just didn't know what to do.

Three days later we went to the adoption agency to pick up our son. The excitement in the car was exhilarating. My mom and I were both crying. My son, Tino, was happy to be getting a baby brother, and my husband was beaming with pride in anticipation of meeting his new son. When we got there, the foster mom who had been taking care of the little boy asked us what we were going to name him, and we told her Joseph. She was thrilled since her daughter always named the boys who came through her care Joey, but no one had kept that name once they were adopted.

I held Joey, and I could tell he was amazing even though I could barely see him through my tears. We took photos with everyone at the agency, including his foster mom, and took our baby home. I loved both my kids the same, and it didn't matter how they'd come to me. I was happy, and my family was complete.

Or so I thought.

SITTING ON A PLANE heading to my next client, I began to write what I thought would be a good start to my book:

> A child is walking through the mist, a lonely soul, thoughtlessly focused on one task, pulling her prized possessions. Wait. Who is that? She's not alone as there are others, each one pulling a red wagon full of their belongings, toys and books. As the fog clears I notice how many there are—hundreds it must be! *Who are these children, and where are they going?* I ask myself. And then it hits me that I am that child; only I'm not five, I'm an adult. *Why am I here, and where am I going?* I look around and notice the others, all adults, neatly dressed in matching suits, all clones of one another, pulling their suitcases behind them. *Oh, I'm here, at the airport. I'm lonely and so tired of the ritual and the routine.*

The book was called *Musings During a Midlife Crisis*, and my plan was to write about my humorous adventures traveling for my job while juggling being a supermom. Only the more I wrote, the more I recognized that I couldn't find anything funny to write about. I was working full-time and living in a hotel in another city most weeks. In the beginning I would cry on the way to the airport, feeling guilty about leaving my kids behind and envious of my husband and mom, who would get to care for them while I was gone.

Over time that changed because when I was home it was as if I didn't exist. Coming home from a long week away, I found that my kids no longer came running to see me at the door when I walked in. They were too busy playing video games with their dad. As I fed them lunch, I got frustrated when they wouldn't eat the peanut butter and jelly sandwiches I had made, and my frustration grew worse when my husband would respond, "They don't like peanut butter and jelly. You don't know what they like. You're never here."

My few days off were spent taking my mom to the doctor for checkups or running errands that my husband hadn't done while I was away. He and I were fighting a lot. "I need to work less," I told him. "I'm exhausted. I want my kids to know who I am! And I can't do that unless you start making more money!"

Then he would yell back, "You need to make sacrifices for the family!"

The situation was my own doing. My husband was narcissistic, selfish, and emotionally abusive. He was also charismatic and charming and told me I was beautiful. He allowed me my independence, something I'd fought for after watching my mom be controlled by my father. Yet in my fight to not become my mother, my life had paralleled hers. I'd married out of convenience after pressure from my parents. I'd had an abortion because the timing wasn't right to have a child. And I was in an abusive marriage.

My husband doesn't hit me, I rationalized, so I enabled his negative behaviors so I could feel good about myself when he put me on a pedestal. I was in a codependent relationship, and I didn't even know what that was at the time. A codependent relationship is an addiction in itself, something I learned as a child from not feeling love from my dad. I was looking for love of myself from the outside, and I enabled the negative behaviors from me and my husband in order to get it. We were no good for each other, but I had known this man since high school. Our relationship was comfortable, and we stuck together, somehow making it work.

The breaking point in our marriage came after I was assigned a job transfer and we moved our family to Colorado. That's when my husband and I started drinking on a regular basis. In Colorado it seemed everyone drank, all the time. I was a social drinker at the time and only drank a couple of drinks every few months. This drinking every day was new to the me of the last few years, but before too long it was like second nature again.

In my hotel room alone I would drink to numb the pain of the boredom of my routine. I was home only one or two days a week, and those days home I was out of sync with my kids. Raising my kids and not raising my kids. I was miserable and started looking for an escape. I had thoughts of disappearing, of not coming home after one of my work trips. I thought my kids would be better off without me. They didn't seem to care if I was home anyway. Their dad was fun. Their dad was there for them. They didn't need me. But I didn't want to leave my kids without their mother.

I was depressed and lonely. I thought about suicide often. *What have I done? How did my life end up like this? Why can't I be happy and grateful for the things I do have in my life? Why me?*

While I was wallowing in my self-pity, my marriage was falling apart. My husband had been recently diagnosed with a medical condition for which the doctor prescribed pain pills, and he started abusing them. In my absence, he found himself a girlfriend and they "played house" with my kids while I was away. My mom tried to warn me about this girl and my husband's behavior. Even though my intuition knew that she was telling the truth, I defended him, telling her they were just friends and to stay out of my business. His girlfriend was a drug addict who enabled him as much as I did. On New Year's Eve I went searching on his computer for evidence, and I found what I was looking for—proof of his affair.

I confronted my husband about the affair, and when he admitted to his wrongdoing, I expelled him to our basement. The next few months were torture for us both since each night I would walk down to the basement in anger, kicking and hitting him until he awoke from his sleep only to interrogate him with a barrage of questions regarding the affair until I felt satisfied with his answers. I questioned whether or not to stay married. I demanded that he go to rehab for his addiction, but ultimately I knew I couldn't forgive him, no matter what. It was different at that point. We had kids, and I didn't want my kids to be around this behavior. After twenty-two years of marriage, I filed for divorce, and my husband moved out.

The day before my son Joey's fifth birthday, I had finished putting together favors for his party, which was being held at an indoor bounce house, and was putting the finishing touches on the Iron Man cake I'd baked for him when the doorbell rang. The divorce papers had been finalized just a few months prior, and my ex-husband was at the door to pick up the kids.

After the kids were packed in the car, things got heated between me and my ex fairly quickly. Our exchanges were always that way. I was angry at him for his drug use and infidelity, and he was angry at me for divorcing him. This was my house since we'd sold our communal home and I had purchased this one on my own. During the move, I had packed several boxes of belongings I had chosen to be his and stacked them in the garage. I told him I wanted him to take his stuff with him.

Our fight escalated as he refused, stating he had no room in the car, and I wouldn't accept that answer. I went back into the house, and a few minutes later he came storming through the front door.

"Don't ever yell at me like that in front of the kids! I deserve respect," he yelled as he hovered over me, screaming in my face.

"You don't deserve respect, you fucking lying piece of shit," I yelled back. "Get the fuck out of my house." I tried to push him out the front door, but he took a step in and closed the door fully behind him. "Get the fuck out of my house," I said, "or I'm calling the police!" Then I kicked him and spit in his face.

He yelled back at me, and I ran across the room to get to the phone as he chased after me. My mom was in the basement, and when she heard the commotion, she came running in to help. She yelled at my ex-husband while I called 911.

Unfortunately, that incident didn't end in my favor. While it was my house, my ex-husband never actually laid a hand on me, and my actions toward him caused me to get arrested. I left in a police car that day while my husband got himself a victim's advocate and a restraining order against me for himself and my kids. And I never made it to my son's birthday party the next day since the restraining order forbade me to be near them.

I hired myself a good attorney and was able to get the charges dropped and regain custody of my kids. My ex-husband went to rehab for his drug addiction, and part of his recovery was making amends for those he had wronged. He called me one morning to tell me he was sorry for all the things that had gone wrong in our marriage and how he had treated me. During that conversation he said something that really stuck with me: "When you get angry, you become that five-year-old little girl who is angry at her dad, and you lash out trying to defend yourself." And he was right.

After my divorce I was drinking a bottle or two of wine alone every night. My mom lived with me at the time, and she basically raised my kids. My mother didn't drive. Never having passed her driver's test due to the language barrier—she couldn't read the street signs—she depended on others to take her around. In exchange for helping me with my kids, I ran her errands, drove her to doctor's appointments, and managed her finances. I had quit my traveling job and took local employment so I could be around for the kids since they were angry at me for divorcing their dad. I was their mother, but one they hardly knew. I needed and wanted to rebuild my relationship with them, but while I was there physically, I wasn't mentally. Drinking and almost reenacting that scene from the movie where Ashley Judd's character has a nervous breakdown, I lost it almost every night. I didn't hit my kids, but I yelled at them a lot and cried a lot.

I would go into the liquor store each night after work and head straight to the top shelf of red wines. *This one makes me angry. This one makes me depressed. This one makes me cry.* I knew them all. *What kind of mood am I in tonight? I'll start with anger and then end on a good cry.* "Two bottles please."

And so on. With bottles ranging in price between twenty-five and forty-five dollars apiece and with me drinking one to two bottles a night, it became an expensive habit. Dozens of empty bottles filled my recycling bin each week as I dragged it out to the curb, hoping my neighbors didn't see the pile and find out what was going on inside my home.

I'd start out by opening a bottle of wine just before getting the kids ready for bed. By the time they were bathed I had drunk my first bottle of wine. One night as they were playing on the floor in front of me, watching TV, my son threw up, and I completely lost it. I started by yelling at him, then crying myself. I was a wreck. Already drunk and staggering, I fell to the floor and then fell again when I tried to get up. I called out to my mom, who found me crying on the floor next to my son. I was drunk as hell, with wine spilled on the floor and both my kids crying. My mom cleaned up the mess and put the kids to bed. I pulled myself together, only to open another bottle of wine. I had lost all control of my life and myself. Again, I was a victim of my circumstances. It was my Groundhog Day.

I started writing in a journal for my kids to read in case I didn't make it out alive. Thoughts of suicide continued to plague my mind. My kids were young. Tino was eight and Joey was only five, but the effect on them was apparent. I wanted them to know how much I loved them even though I couldn't give them the love and support they needed from me.

9/2-Dear Tino and Joey, I love you more than you will ever know or feel. I do love you so much that it hurts, yet I can't show you, I don't know why—

You don't know me. I'm your mom and you want and need so much from me. I sit in my room drinking and think of you. I hear you, but I can't move. I can't get up. I drown myself in distractions. I'm sitting here drunk on wine, feeling sad and sorry for myself. Why?—

I need help, but I'm too proud or scared to ask for it. I'm struggling, kids. I'm giving you a house and a home, but it's not what you want or need. You need love. You need emotional support and I have none to give.

I only had the kids part-time each week, and on the days I didn't have them, I went out with single friends until the early-morning hours to the bars—drinking, dancing, and fitting in a few one-night stands in between. I barely slept. I powered on in a fog. I did anything to escape from my own reality.

On the rare nights I sat home alone with no kids or friends to hang out with, I drank on the couch, screaming at no one, "I'm so fucking bored!"

A friend of mine owned a restaurant, and I'd spend hours there drinking just for something to do. I even tried pot and cocaine again a few times at the coercion of a friend but ultimately decided they weren't for me. I was grateful that I hadn't fallen completely back into my old ways, or so I thought, but I still had alcohol, and I was back to being comfortably numb. I hated my life.

When my younger son, Joey, was small, I was the one he was most attached to, and yet as I became more absorbed in my personal misery, he showed me in his own way how I hadn't been there for him. One day he came home from school with a gift he'd made at school. It was a turkey traced from his hand, and on each feather he'd named a person he was thankful for. As I read each feather, I saw that he had chosen to leave me off of it. I was hurt.

I asked him why he hadn't put my name on his artwork, and he just said, "I don't know." I asked him again, and he said, "I don't like you".

Tino smiled and gave me a hug. "We're thankful for you, Mommy!"

But it was too late. The pain I felt had already been inflicted. I started drinking soon after. I sulked in my room, feeling unloved again—this time by my own son. When I came out of my room, I walked downstairs to see stacks of my books tossed on the floor. Tino was standing on top of them.

"What the fuck are you doing? Get off my fucking books! Why would you throw all my fucking books on the floor?" He was only eight years old, and yet I completely lost it. I continued to yell at him. I called him selfish and sent him to his room. Once he was there, I raced after him and flung the door open. I grabbed each book off his bookshelf and tossed each one by one across his room, screaming at him the entire time. "How do you fucking like this, huh? Do you like your fucking books being thrown around? How does it fucking feel?"

When I was done, I yelled, "Clean up this fucking mess!" and stormed out. I was awful. My behavior terrified him. I could tell. I went back into my bedroom and cried so hard, thinking how I had turned into my father. I poured myself another glass of wine and fell asleep. While I didn't hit my kids, I yelled at them and instilled the same anger and fear that my father had imprinted on me. I was struggling, and my kids were paying the price. I judged myself for how I was raising them and then drank to hide from the overwhelming guilt I put on myself.

11/19 - Today Joey came home with a homemade turkey. Each of the feathers had something to be thankful for. One was Dad, one was Tino, one was our pets and one was Grandma—I wasn't on there. He told me it was because he didn't like me.

Boy that hurt. Tino, you stuck up for me. I shouldn't burden you with this, but later I got angry and took it out on you. Tino, you got in trouble tonight. You trashed my books for no reason. I trashed yours in return while yelling and screaming at you. I ignored you both tonight; I was so mad. I'm not a good mom. I'm so confused, but you are just kids. I'm hating life right now. I want to run away. I love you so much, but I am so overwhelmed, so tired. I suck as a mom.

It's so hard to write, but I fear I may not be around for you. I drink. I'm sick. I'm depressed. I hope you grow older and will be strong. I can't be. I want to disappear. No one knows this. I can't be strong any longer. God help me—

Tino cleaned up his room and later apologized to me for trashing my books, but it didn't matter—the damage had been done.

I worked with a man who was very religious. He prayed with me and told me the story of Job. I was Job, he said, and one day I would find happiness and riches beyond my imagination. I just needed to be patient. While I had given up on God a long time before, I felt I had nothing to lose, so I prayed with him and hoped that he was right.

I didn't mind when he or anyone prayed for me even if I didn't believe in God—how could I believe when I was always suffering? What had God done for me? I viewed my life in those broken chapters by this time: child abuse, drug abuse, infertility, and, lastly, divorce. Admitting that was progress for me, and I started telling my story, *sort of*. At the least I gave away the titles of these chapters even if I hid the details behind them, still ashamed. It felt freeing to talk about them with my coworkers or a friend. Each time a small weight lifted. Each chapter was a badge earned and my excuse for being miserable.

The drinking and lack of sleep were taking their toll on me. I had always had issues with sleep, staying up at night and hiding under the covers as I did as a child, wide awake so I could be ready for when my dad came back to "kill me in my sleep."

The drinking helped me ease my pain, and it also helped me sleep. I was alone in a big house, my kids were in the other room or at their father's house, and my mom was sleeping in her apartment in the basement. I had sleepless nights, and I was afraid to sleep. My childhood nightmares had returned—those recurring dreams of the boy dying in a well, the soldier on the battlefield, and the peasant woman dying in a fire along with her village. Most of them were reruns from my earlier days as a child, but some were new. I dreaded going to sleep since I feared what I might encounter. As I lay down, I became that frightened little girl each night—hiding under the blanket, covers over my head, curled up in a ball, in fear just the way I'd feared my dad, only this time I was in fear of my own tortured self.

It was also during this time that I started having visitations from spirits—and that brought me to question my sanity.

Each night as I lay there, I could feel the presence of a man watching over me. He was angry at me. I yelled from under the safety of my covers, "Go away! Leave me alone." I hid there until I fell asleep, only to be woken up by a terrible nightmare. Then he was gone, but he was persistent and kept coming back.

He would come out at night as I walked the hallways of my home. I could feel him near me, and without sound he would tell me this was his house and that I needed to leave. I kept this experience to myself since I didn't want people to think I was crazy. I started praying at night to anyone who would listen, asking if there was a God to protect me.

Maybe this man who came to visit me was my imagination or a hallucination from the alcohol, or maybe I was going crazy. The nightmares as a child, the visions of the past—could they have all been self-induced? I was starting to think that all those years of experiences like this one were the result of my mind playing tricks on me and that I was literally, certifiably crazy. You see, it wasn't the first time I'd been visited by such a presence.

When I was twenty-five and living in a house in New York that I'd purchased with my then-husband, I awoke one night to find an old man kneeling by my bedside praying. He was right next to me, but he was praying to his sick wife. I think he thought that I was her. I was frightened and asked him to go away. I pulled the covers over my head, terrified, until I finally fell asleep. I knew when we bought the house that it had been abandoned. It had been lived in by an older couple. The wife died in the home, followed by her husband years later. Their kids had held onto the house, which sat empty for an entire year before we purchased it.

Years later I was living in a house in Las Vegas, right near a cemetery. One time while I was in my bathroom, I felt someone staring at me as I was getting ready in the mirror. I turned slowly to see a young boy standing alone in my bathroom watching me. I couldn't actually *see* him, but I could feel his presence. I could tell he was a boy of about fourteen. It gave me chills. As quickly as he'd appeared, once I asked him to leave, he disappeared. Often

I would wake up to an older man or some other figure standing at the end of my bed. Once again, I would lie there, covers over my head, trying to close my mind so the man's spirit wouldn't take mine over.

"Go away," I would tell them. I didn't understand them, so to me they were evil. I didn't want them penetrating my soul. These experiences left me unsettled, and I would try to block them from my mind whenever they happened. *Don't think about it. Do something else. Block your thoughts. It's not real.*

I was terrified of these spirits, yet I never told anyone about them lest they think I was crazy. The few times I told my then-husband about my experiences with spirits, he told me it was neurological and all in my head. I read that as his way of saying I was crazy. I was so sure they were spirits, but I questioned myself always. *Is it me? Am I crazy?* These experiences were real to me, but not wanting to be told I was crazy, I stopped talking about them.

Then six months after the divorce, I was losing it. *Maybe it's the alcohol? Maybe my mind is playing tricks on me? Maybe I really am crazy?* My thoughts haunted me as did this man. There was another entity that would also appear, an evil presence that was half man, half gargoyle. He would sit on top of the shelf in my bedroom. "Go away!" I would yell at him. Under the safety of my blankets, I would then pray to God or the Devil, whoever was presenting this threat to me, to go away and leave me alone.

What if God did exist? Were the spirits payback for the horrible person I was in this life? Was the Devil responsible for all the other visions I had experienced that terrified me, when I'd lie awake at night trying so hard to keep my mind closed so the evil spirits wouldn't enter me? I was a mental case, and I could let no one know lest that person think I was crazy. I didn't trust in God, and I had no one on earth to turn to.

Each day I went to work exhausted but functioning. In the evenings I hung out with friends and acted as if nothing was wrong. Once I got home, though, I lived in fear of the night. I drank more to ensure I passed out without encountering any spirits.

The old man persisted and even started playing tricks on me. Lights would go on and off in the house, mostly in my bedroom or the upstairs hallways. "Stop it!" I would yell, and he'd turn them on again. I tried to rationalize these events. I read all about similar experiences on the internet. I read that women going through menopause could create these occurrences in the house. I was in my forties—perhaps this was the answer. Was I creating this in my mind because of my anger at my dad, my divorce, or life itself? Maybe I only knew how to live in fear? Or maybe I was just a mental case.

And then it started happening to my kids. Lights going on and off at will. It scared them. I hired an electrician to see if there was something wrong with the wiring, but he found nothing. I joked with the kids and my mom that there was a ghost living in the house, but I never told them I really believed that. I never told them how fearful I was of this man or how worried I was for my own sanity.

After about a year of living in this house, I was talking with a neighbor of mine. She didn't know what I had been experiencing. I asked her about the previous owners. She told me that the original owner, which was two owners prior, had fallen off a ladder in front of the house, gone to bed in my bedroom, and died there. My heart stopped. I finally understood.

When we first moved into the house, I had hired contractors to remodel the basement so my mom could have her own master bedroom and living quarters. The space had been remodeled before, but only as a do-it-yourself project. The owner had filed a permit with the city and then done the work himself. He tore down walls, did the electrical work himself, and added a bathroom. I was convinced that our remodel had somehow brought his spirit out. I finally told my mom about the man in the house and my experiences with him. She didn't see or feel the spirits, but she believed me. She told me that her mom would talk to ghosts all the time. OK, so either my grandmother was also crazy and that's where I got it from, or this stuff was for real.

One night my older son woke up in the middle of the night and called for me. I went into his room. He was scared. "I woke up and there was a man standing over my bed watching me," he said. I asked him if he was still there, and he said, "No, when I called you the man left through the window, and then I heard a car door slam, and the lights drove off." Another night, the kids were in their rooms playing when they came out yelling that the lights had gone out on their own.

The old man had started making his way through the house. What had begun in my bedroom now moved through the hallways and my kids' rooms and then throughout the house. Then my mom started having similar experiences in the basement, with lights going on and off at will. She would calmly walk upstairs and say, "Marisa, I think the ghost is in our basement now!" She would have a confused look on her face, hoping I had some answers. We were all affected, but we joked about it with the kids since we didn't want them to be scared. My mom and I would ease their minds by telling them the ghost was fake, that the lights flickering was due to bad electrical wiring, even though we believed the ghost was real.

During this time, we also had a lot of issues with our internet service. The internet was always going out, and I was constantly calling our provider to fix it. We had old phone jacks in the house, one in the living room and one in my son's room. The internet was connected through the phone jacks. At one point the serviceman for our internet provider recommended that we disconnect the phone jacks and route the internet cables differently, so I agreed. It seemed to work to fix the issue.

My kids were at their dad's house when I got the internet cable rerouted. That first night upon their return, my older son woke up in the middle of the night from a bad dream. In the dream, he was at his dad's house and a ghost was chasing his family. They locked themselves behind a door, and the ghost kept banging on the door asking for his phone back.

When my son told me this, chills ran down my entire body. I panicked. One of the phone jacks we'd turned off was in his room, and this was now the second time this spirit had tried to interact with my son. I lay down with him in his bed, told him it was just a dream, and stayed with him until he fell asleep. To him, it was just a dream that he didn't even remember the next day. As for myself, however, it had sent a fear creeping through me like I had never felt before.

The next day I called our internet provider and requested that the jacks be turned back on. I didn't know what to do. I couldn't move again. That would be too expensive, and a move was not something I was ready to take on anyway. *What the hell is going on? What am I going to do?* I was scared. I knew it was me who had brought these spirits into our lives—I had experienced this my whole life—but I had no idea why or how to control it, and I had no one to talk to about it.

I did mention it to a friend, who recommended a medium who could help me perform a cleansing in the house to rid ourselves of the ghost's presence. One night some friends joined me and our medium to see if we could connect to this man. We started by "smudging"—which in this instance meant burning sage to purify the air—and then preparing the room. When I sat down on the couch, I felt a coldness and a presence near me. I instantly got chills.

He's back, I thought. I didn't say anything about it since I wanted to see if this woman was for real or, possibly, to see if I was crazy. The woman who came to perform the cleansing looked at me at the same instant I felt his presence. She said, "I see him. He's sitting right next to you." I was scared, but I was also relieved to find out that I wasn't crazy. I spoke directly to him: "This is no longer your house." I told him that I lived there with my mom and kids and that it was my house now and that he had to leave. Our medium then spoke to him and helped him cross over, to look for the light, and I felt him leave.

The night of the cleansing I was confident that he was gone, but I still lived in fear that he would return. And while the old man did not come back, the half-man-half-gargoyle creature continued to appear, always at the end of my bed or sitting atop my bedroom shelf, staring at me until I yelled for him to leave. Each time I questioned my sanity. Each time I was instilled with more fear. I looked up every possible explanation for these experiences, looking for the answer that explained I wasn't crazy, but I never found what I was looking for. Instead, I spent each night drinking, drowning out my emotions and fears as I locked the door to my bedroom and tried to find some feeling of safety in my own home.

Those experiences in the years around my divorce led me to realize how broken I really was. I was living in anger and resentment toward my family. I struggled with playing my role as a mom, a daughter, and an employee at work. I was tired of raising my kids and supporting my mom, giving so much of myself to others that it seemed like everyone around me was sucking the life out of me. I felt bad for my kids since I knew I wasn't emotionally there for them, but I was screaming inside. I was alone and going through the motions of life. I had tried to be strong my entire life, in order to protect myself and my siblings as a young child and after the divorce to help my kids and my mom. I had to keep it together for everyone else while ignoring my own needs.

As a child I had been terrified to sleep at night because of my dad and my nightmares. Nothing had changed as an adult. My nightmares had returned, and I had spirits hounding me in my house. At forty-five years old, I was terrified and once again sleeping under the covers in a fetal position just as I had done as a child. On the outside I looked perfectly normal. I had a good job, friends, kids, and a good life. Yet each night I drank to keep myself numb and stumbled around my house yelling, "Why me? Why can't I just feel normal? I'm a fucking nut job! God, please help. Someone, please?" Until I eventually cried myself to sleep.

2

MY BODY IS A BURDEN

AT THE END OF MY fifth-grade year, I passed around an autograph book to my friends so they could sign it. On one of the first few pages of the book was a place to list my favorite things and my personal motto. For my motto I wrote, "Always eat and you'll feel great." Despite my early dinner-table battles with my dad, I loved food and ate a lot of it. I was a skinny kid, and I could eat for two or three at every meal. Funny thing was, as much as I loved food, it didn't love me back.

Being a victim puts a strain on your physical self. Since I spent most of my life focusing on survival, I would never really take care of myself. When I was focusing on all the drama in my life, I would move forward by distracting myself with work, alcohol, and taking care of family, and I would ignore myself and my own needs. Whenever I would become ill, I would turn to doctors to give me my quick fix. My entire life I had been wrought with sickness, and just as I was a functioning abuser, I would become a functioning sick person.

In my Sicilian family when I was a child, our family ate a lot of homemade pasta, breads, sauces, and cookies. I loved all of it—the homemade bread, the lasagna, and the biscotti (Italian cookies), which I would dunk in milk or tea and which would melt on my tongue as I put them in my mouth. So delicious this food was!

Yet after many meals, and especially during holidays or special occasions when I had overindulged, my family would find me in my bedroom, facedown on my bed with a pillow against my stomach, moaning in pain. My stomach hurt, and my back hurt, and I was in dire pain. During the few times my family took me to the emergency room, I was given pain meds to ease the pain, but no doctor knew what was causing it.

My symptoms were always the same: severe stomach pain as if my insides were rotting and burning with fire; stabbing lower back pain so sharp that I swore I had broken bones; diarrhea; bloating; gas pains; and headaches. During these moments I would think my father had broken me somehow from all his hitting. I blamed him for my sickness.

I also broke out in skin rashes quite a bit. I had what looked like large white cauliflowers on both my ankles, and they constantly itched. I scratched and tore at those things until they bled. For my sisters and parents, it was just another thing they could yell at me for, but I couldn't help it. I needed to stop the itching, and I didn't care if it bled.

I broke out with red bumps and marks on my face often. My sister would call them "my diseases" when they would crop up on my face out of the blue. I had such sensitive skin that even popping a pimple would cause a burn on my face. When I was twelve, my parents took me to get braces. When the dentist made an impression of my teeth to make a little cast of my current teeth, some of the impression mixture got on my top lip. It burned the top of my lip and damaged the nerves. It left a scar, which at the time I thought was so cool because I looked like Lindsay Wagner from *The Bionic Woman*, a hero of mine as a kid. While the scar is no longer visible, I still get little twitches on my lip where the damage occurred.

My parents didn't care—or that is what I thought. They took me to doctors for my maladies, but doctors were expensive, so it wasn't often, especially since the doctors could never diagnose my illnesses. I was too young to understand why I was so sick, and so it was easy to just blame my dad since I hated him anyway.

My body is a burden. I've thought this most of my life. Over time I was no longer comfortable in my own skin. Each time I would eat, use a new soap, or, later on, makeup, I'd psych myself up to prepare for whatever symptoms would follow. I hated the ritual: *OK, I need to eat. That lasagna is so good. Just one bite. Just eat a small piece. Maybe this time I won't get sick. If I eat it without drinking water I should feel OK—no, wait, I'll eat, then wait two hours, then drink water. I think that helped. I can't remember—what did I do last time?*

Then once I ate, the pain would slowly come. While lying in bed, I would start to hate myself for taking a bite. *I shouldn't have eaten that. I only waited an hour before I drank water. It might have worked if I hadn't had that second piece. I should have waited the two hours. Fuck! I hate my dad. He did this to me. He fucking broke me, and now I'm suffering. God, I hate my life!*

In my twenties I found a doctor who diagnosed me with ulcers, and I spent many years going to the gastroenterologist and taking ulcer medication. While it helped sometimes, I used to beg my doctor to take out my intestines since the pain was unbearable. I'm glad he refused.

Around the same time, I was also diagnosed with Graves' disease, a thyroid disorder where your body starts to reject your thyroid as if it's a foreign object. My thyroid had gone into overdrive and was causing heart palpitations and making my hands shake and my hair fall out. After seeing a specialist, it was recommended that I kill my thyroid using radiation treatment. I agreed because I didn't know any better.

The day I went for treatment was surreal. My doctor walked me into a room where he wore a gown and matching hat made of the heavy materials you wear when you are at the dentist getting X-rays. With gloves made of the same material, he opened a very large metal canister with a skull and crossbones poison symbol on it. Using a long set of tongs, he reached into the canister and slowly pulled out what looked like a huge pill and handed it to me. I did not have the luxury of wearing his outfit as he offered this pill to me, and I accepted it barehanded. He seemed panicked that I didn't hold it over the sink in the room and made me reach over the sink should I drop this pill full of poison.

I looked at it, took a deep breath, and popped it into my mouth. I drank water, and down it went. My instructions were to go home and stay away from young kids for a few days to avoid contaminating them. A few weeks later I came back for a follow-up visit, and my thyroid had shrunk down to nothing.

Since then I have taken a thyroid medication to stabilize my metabolism. If I go a few days without it, my body starts to cramp up and slowly slow down. I've been told I have to take this medication for the rest of my life. Some days I wonder what I would do if there were an apocalypse and I didn't have access to it.

I had no control over my body and the havoc it wreaked on me. In my mind I still blamed all my problems on my dad, who I thought had broken me when I was young and had caused all my sicknesses.

In my thirties, scientists announced that ulcers were caused by a type of bacteria. *Yay! I'll be cured!* Only it was the one type of bacteria that I didn't have. So the mystery was not solved after all. I stopped the ulcer medications and continued with my pain. I started to recognize that certain foods would be triggers, and some would actually ease the pain. Red onions and swiss cheese gave me migraines, so I stayed away from them. If I ate pretzels or saltines, they had to be unsalted because the salted ones would burn my stomach. If I happened to go for a run, I noticed my symptoms would disappear. So to keep moving, if it was too late at night to go outside, I took to jogging in place around my house. Occasionally, when the pain was unbearable, I would drive myself to the hospital and get a shot of pain meds. I went alone several times since I was the only person I could count on. I was strong, independent, and self-sufficient. I was a survivor. I didn't need anyone to cater to me since I had been my only support for as long as I could remember.

Being that I was sick all the time, I used to read a lot of magazines about health. Also, being a science fiction nerd and tech geek, I read *Discover* magazine quite a bit. In the back of the magazine was a column called "Vital Signs" that featured someone who had an illness who'd spent an entire life going to multiple doctors with no one able to find a cure. I was looking for *my cure, my fix,* in every word I read. I was searching for the answer to all my illnesses. The columns were eventually collected into a book called *Discover Magazine's Vital Signs: True Tales of Medical Mysteries, Obscure Diseases, and Life-Saving Diagnoses.* I read the magazine. I read the column faithfully each month, but I never saw a story that sounded like mine.

One day, though, I was watching a TV show with a similar theme, and it happened! *Eureka! That's me!* A woman was reenacting my life exactly on the screen. I couldn't believe it. The episode was about porphyria, a condition that caused severe pain somewhat alleviated by being active and eating carbs. This disease described my symptoms exactly.

I was thrilled to finally discover what I had, and I even found a gastroenterologist who would listen to me. He provided me a prescription for an antispasmodic, which I would use whenever I felt the pain coming on. This helped me quite a bit over the years, but still it wasn't a cure. It was like eating Tums after a hot chili burrito. I was fixing the symptoms but not the cause.

A few years later, when the pain was again unbearable, I had my gallbladder removed as recommended by my doctor, but again, it was a temporary fix. Food continued to be a mental mindfuck for me. I thought about it constantly—what I could or couldn't eat.

I was trying to help myself, but I didn't understand anything about food and nutrition. My mindset was to just fix the symptoms. I knew the cause—the cause was my father making me sick with his physical beatings.

My physical self was a burden on me. I no longer enjoyed eating because I almost always got sick soon after. It was my new normal. I spent a lot of time in the bathroom. *What a waste of time this is.* I thought about how much time we spend feeding our bodies and then peeing and pooing to get rid of what we just ate. The monotony of it all is laughable if you think about it, and I thought about it a lot.

Over the years I began to think of my body as detached or separate from who I was. A burden in so many ways. I had food and stomach issues. I had sensitive skin. I had dyslexia. I had and still have obsessive-compulsive disorder issues where I check and recheck locks and stoves, count and recount, and fidget—my mind never at ease, always thinking about how my body was never on the same page as the rest of my environment. I spent so much of my thought process every day being afraid—of eating, of getting sick, of washing my clothes and getting itchy, of trying new makeup and breaking out, or of having my face burn from a new lotion.

And then sleep. *Boy, do I love sleep!* I could sleep for twelve hours straight when I did fall asleep, and I took naps often to keep up when I didn't. I was always trying to supercharge myself in between the demands of my hectic life. The problem was that my sleep was not always good. Besides the nightmares of my past, I've also had episodes of sleep paralysis, waking up paralyzed in my bed and trying to scream as loud as I could to get someone's attention or to make myself wake up completely. I used to stress about going to sleep because I was afraid of the nightmares or spending the night tossing and turning all night, being restless and not able to sleep, my mind never calm with all the nonsense in my head.

I've had fourteen surgeries in my life, and I was always of the thought that whatever was wrong with me, like a car, I could just go in and "fix it." I've had two knee surgeries, a foot surgery, five infertility-related surgeries, Achilles surgery, Lasix eye surgery, and nose surgery after I broke my nose and had severe headaches from it, gallbladder removal, installation of a bladder sling after my bladder dropped from my six pregnancies, and a C-section. I never had any idea how to care for myself.

I wasn't a hypochondriac—I never complained to anyone about my illnesses, and the pain was real. I kept my health issues mostly to myself. I was too proud and too strong to complain about it. I didn't want to come across as weak. I sucked it up and pushed through the day-to-day, but it was a total mindfuck for me.

After my divorce, I put on over thirty pounds from all the drinking. I had stopped running because my knee was giving me trouble. My only forms of exercise were hiking and walking since those cleared my head. I wasn't healthy, and I was taking blood pressure medication since the stress of my divorce was taking its toll on me. *WTF? Is this how everyone lives?* I just wanted to be free of so much thought around this heavy burden I carried around. Physically and mentally I was a mess, and it was catching up to me.

3

TRANSFORMATION

IT WAS AFTER MY DIVORCE as I arrived home at five in the morning from a night out. My mom was sitting at the kitchen table. She smiled as I walked in. I was disheveled and holding my stilettos in my hand. She was excited to hear how my date had gone. It was a blind date with a lawyer my girlfriend had set me up with. The night had started out as dinner at a friend's restaurant. My words stumbled as I tried to tell my mom about it. I was still drunk.

"We went to dinner; then we started drinking heavily. When the restaurant closed, we had sex in the restaurant. Then we went dancing, and I had sex in the bar with him. I don't know what the fuck I was thinking, Mom."

She looked at me, and in a very nonjudgmental way, she said, "Don't beat yourself up. You did what you did. Just let it go." I went up to bed and fell asleep.

I woke up in a panic. *What was I thinking? What the fuck is wrong with me? What if someone had recorded me with a phone?* I sat in my bedroom and cried all day. I needed to change. I couldn't continue living the way I was.

In that moment, as I reviewed my life, I realized that I had never truly been happy. My life had been defined in those four chapters: child abuse, drug and alcohol abuse, infertility, divorce. I only saw the negativity in my life. I was playing the role of a victim. Even the success I'd had with work was a failure to me because I was a workaholic. I'd strived so hard to succeed, but it dawned on me that this was also an addiction, playing into my false sense of worth that I allowed in my life to fill the emptiness inside of me.

I was terrified day and night, scared that I knew nothing of myself except that I was a hot mess. I had no control over my drinking or my mind. My mind was clouded with judgment of myself and others and anger toward anyone and anything. I lived in fear of both the human and spiritual world.

Lost and out of control, I needed something more. I needed to take control of myself, my mind, and my soul. It was time to look deep into my failures and take responsibility for my happiness and own it! I needed to heal. I wanted to know what it was like to be happy. I wanted to be in a place where my mind was at peace.

It was time for a change, and I was finally ready.

At this point I was physically and mentally broken. I needed to fix myself badly from the core of my soul, and I had no idea where to begin. In my twenties I had read books by Alan Watts and Carlos Castaneda and tried to find enlightenment, but my victim-thinking consumed my thoughts. More recently, I turned to self-help books and practiced yoga and meditation to clear my head. It worked as long as I was in the moment of these practices, but the rest of the day I was back to my old self. I wanted to feel that peace all the time.

I googled the word "transformation," and the following definition appeared: "a thorough or dramatic change in form or appearance." I wanted a dramatic change desperately, and I knew I had to take extreme measures to fix myself. But I had no idea where to begin.

The longest road for me was admitting defeat. That was the toughest challenge I had ever taken on in my lifetime. In the past, when I'd known I had some emotional issues and I'd tried a few self-help books and several therapists to help me through them, I'd only scraped the surface from the outside in. This time was different. This time I knew every cell of mine needed to be torn apart and rebuilt.

I had been watching Joel Osteen's show with my mom on Sundays and seen the inspiration he brought to so many people. I still didn't believe in God, but Osteen's stories of real-life people overcoming their obstacles resonated with me. I watched Oprah, Dr. Oz, Deepak Chopra—they all believed in themselves and shared messages of hope. I wanted to be like them, but inside I was so broken. I felt like those around me knew I was a fake. I had no messages of hope. I was on the other side, still struggling with my demons. Something had to change, and that change had to come from within, from deep inside my core. From the inside out, not the other way around. I was ready, and I was up for the challenge.

After hours of crying and wondering why my life's journey had brought me to this place, I pushed aside my self-pity and made my announcement out loud: "Today I'm making a 100 percent commitment to heal myself. I want to know what it's like to be happy." No one heard me except for my dog, but saying it out loud was my promise to myself that it had to be done. I'd do whatever it took to really and truly heal myself from my core. From the broken little girl inside of me to the seemingly adult and outwardly confident woman that I was, I was going to open myself up, examine every bit of me, and fix what was broken to find that happiness. I didn't know how I was going to do it, but for the first time in my life I was confident I was going to figure it out. I stopped crying, and a calmness set in as I pulled the covers over my head and went back to sleep for the remainder of the day.

The next few days I went online looking for information about how I could start my transformation. In addition to "transformation," I googled the words "self-help" and "happiness," reading any article that resonated with me. As I continued my search, I came across several articles that intrigued me. They all had some recurring themes in common. I finally knew what my first step would be.

The first thing I did was go out and get two large tattoos to signify my commitment. It's probably not what most people would consider a first step, but for me it was life changing. By tattooing on myself a symbol of where I wanted to be in my life, I would be consistently reminded of my goal. I found a tattoo parlor and planned my design with a young artist. I had brought photos of a lotus flower, a dove, the symbol for om (in Hinduism and other religions chiefly of India, om is an ancient sacred symbol also represented by sounds), and a cherry blossom tree. In my research looking for my symbols of hope, these were images that I'd connected with.

During two five-hour sessions, I was transformed physically, my commitment set in ink as a reminder of my quest. On my back, taking up the entire top right of my shoulder, was now a large cherry blossom tree. In the Chinese culture, the cherry blossom tree symbolizes the strong feminine woman. In Japanese culture, it represents the fragility and the beauty of life but also a time for renewal. For me, this tattoo meant strength and rejuvenation and a time for change—a woman transformed. Having it placed on my back meant it would support and carry me forward while leaving the broken parts behind.

The other tattoo was just below my left rib, ending at my hip. I put it there so every day when I looked in the mirror it would remind me of my commitment to myself. It is a lotus flower with the om symbol in the middle. Above it rises a dove holding tightly in its wings a large red heart. I had read about the lotus flower, which starts as a seed from the bottom of a muddy pond and, fighting all obstacles, emerges to the surface a beautiful flower. I was that lotus seed at the bottom of that dark pond, and I wanted to bloom. My way out was discovering who I really was, my true self. Through this discovery, I could find peace and understand the mysteries of the universe that have haunted me most of my life.

In my tattoo, I represented that peace and understanding with the symbol of om. The om symbol represents the various states of consciousness and chanting the om sounds is said to bring one peace and bliss, and a connection with the Divine. I wanted so badly to emerge from that pond surrounded by the love of God and, more importantly, myself. In my tattoo, the dove represented God, and the heart was me. Every day I looked in the mirror and hoped that one day I would feel what my tattoo represented, but for the moment, I knew I had a long way to go.

My next step was to continue my research. What did I need to do to get happy? What did others do to get happy? I started reading a lot of books. I was drawn to books about spirituality, past lives, and finding happiness. Books on God, the universe, and understanding my place in this crazy world.

A friend of mine had taken me to my first yoga class shortly after I'd separated from my husband. During the class I felt a vulnerability I had never felt before, and tears streamed down my face as I tried to focus on the poses. I didn't realize I was crying until my girlfriend handed me a tissue. I connected to that experience of vulnerability and peace I'd felt almost instantly in that first class. Yoga has been around for centuries and is a practice of slow movements and poses known to enhance your health with both physical and mental benefits. I never liked the thought of exercise or gyms, and yoga was nothing like that. It made me feel like I was taking care of my mind and myself, and it was really helping me. I practiced yoga regularly through those years and started up a more regular practice at home. Just fifteen or twenty minutes a day each morning, a few days a week, was all it took for me to start feeling calm and in tune with myself.

Part of yoga includes the practice of meditation during the exercises. I enjoyed these small meditations during class since they were the times when I felt the most calm. Over the years I had tried meditating, mostly at night to help me sleep, but at this point I was buying books on how to properly meditate. At first it was difficult. I couldn't clear my mind, and I got frustrated that I couldn't find that euphoria I had read about in books, that elevated state of being that people experienced when they meditated.

But then I figured it out. I was sitting in meditation, and my focus was all over the place. My thoughts continued to revolve around beating myself up: *You're a bad person. You're mean. You're selfish. You're a terrible mom.* My dad kept coming up, along with my angry feelings for him. These thoughts raced through my mind, and I kept trying to push them aside. *Focus— you can do this. Don't listen to those words.* But the words kept coming back, forcing their hatred of me into my mind until finally I gave up and thought this: *Let me just listen.* And once I did, a whole new door opened up for me and my healing.

Accept it. Feel it. Dissolve it. Expand.

It was that simple. I listened to the thoughts that came through. It didn't matter if I was thinking about my grocery list, whom I was angry at, or my frustration that I couldn't meditate. I accepted my thoughts without judgment and let my mind go. My thoughts would wander but then ultimately come back to why I was there, what I was searching for. Memories in my chapters would appear, and I would just acknowledge that the events had happened and accept them for what they were.

Once I accepted each thought and allowed it to remain, I tried to put a feeling to it. Did this thought make me angry, sad, or depressed? Did it make me happy? Usually my first emotion toward a thought was what I called a surface emotion. It really wasn't why it decided to enter my head. I knew it was a fake, and I had to break it apart to find out what the true emotion really was.

And that's when I would dissolve it and solve it. Dissolving it meant that I tried to determine why I was feeling the emotion that was attached to the thought. Was I really feeling angry? I dug deeper, and asked myself more questions. My feelings were not anger at my dad for beating me—I was sad and hurt that he didn't love me. And breaking it apart even more, I could figure out that I felt unloved.

Once I uncovered what the issue really was, I could expand my mind toward actions. With regard to my dad, how could I build a more loving relationship with him in the present instead of focusing on our past together? What actions could I take to feel loved on my terms without allowing someone else to be responsible for my feelings of being loved? How could I love myself? Sorting through these questions was key in taking steps toward my growth.

"Dissolve it and solve it"—using these words was a simplistic way of describing my method for figuring out how to meditate, but it worked. Solving my attachments to the negative thoughts and emotions brought me peace. That's because once I solved my thought, the chatter in my mind would disappear, leaving a world of calmness. I could move on during my meditation and welcome any experiences that would come afterward. And putting the thoughts away brought forth emotions beyond anything I could have imagined. Each meditation brought me clarity, resolution, and most importantly, direction.

Meditation, even just a few minutes a day, was like going to a therapist for me—only I knew what questions to ask myself. The process was simple, and it allowed me to think and say anything that came to mind without judgment of myself or my answers. I began trusting myself and my thoughts. Instead of the negative self-talk I was used to, I turned to meditation to listen to myself for guidance.

I started learning more and found out there are all kinds of meditation. I bought relaxation CDs to play in my car such as *Tao: Music for Relaxation* by Ron Allen & One Sky. I meditated to visualization CDs like *Morning Glory—Mastering Manifestations,* guided by Lilian B. Eden, and *The Practice of Tibetan Meditation* by Dagsay Tulku Rinpoche. When I picked up the book *The Long Road Turns to Joy, A Guide to Walking Meditation* by Thich Nhat Hanh, I found that walking meditations were my favorite since they helped me be more mindful of each step, of myself, and of my surroundings.

I was reading books on how to calm the mind and find peace. I had an empty bedroom that I painted the color of melting chocolate and converted to my "Zen room," where I practiced my yoga and meditation. I was in there a lot—reading, listening, doing—and it was working. My mind was getting clearer, and I was learning a lot about myself. I realized that I was my own worst enemy in how I judged myself. My mantra of *Why me?*—grown from the pain I'd endured as a child—had led me to a lifetime of playing the role of a victim. If I was going to find happiness, I had to let that mindset go.

I had always enjoyed running, hiking, and walking in the past since these activities raised my serotonin levels and helped calm my mind, so I did more of them whenever I could. It was during this time that I became more aware that when I was mentally healthy, I was motivated to continue the activities that were calming to me and less apt to drink, smoke, or eat unhealthily. I tried to do one healthy thing each day, even if it was only a few minutes—a meditation in the morning, a hike in the afternoon, or a walk after work. Each time I did that, I felt better about myself.

Being more confident that I was on the road to recovery, I started talking about my past. Those boxes had been taken out of the closet, and now I unlocked them. The details of the chapters came out in talks with anyone who was ready to listen. Talking about them was freeing. I was an open book. I talked to my girlfriends about how unhappy I had been and the sadness and depression I struggled with. I talked with my mom a lot about my feelings of wanting to disappear, about feeling like I was a bad mom. I stopped hiding behind the chapters. I finally felt no shame, no self-judgment about my past, and I didn't care if others judged me. I talked about my abusive childhood, my escape with drugs and alcohol, my infertility, and my divorce. Some of my friends were surprised since it seemed like I had my life together. Once I opened up to them, I found out that they could relate and had stories of their own.

My dark past that I'd hidden for years, fearing I would be found to be a fraud, had only been keeping me from finding my happiness. The more I let those chapters go, the happier and more peaceful I became.

During this time a friend suggested that I go to church with her, and I did. I hadn't been to mass in a long time, though I had visited many churches in between. I had always loved churches, even if I didn't go to mass, and when I traveled, I enjoyed going to churches in different cities to view their architecture. Churches are so beautiful, especially the very old ones. I appreciate the stained-glass windows, the altars, the beautiful pews. Yet something about them was also unnerving. I was a bad kid, remember?

God hadn't answered my prayers as a young child, the desperate pleas, seemingly motivated by the Devil, wishing my dad would die. I would walk up to the statues of Jesus or Mary and perform the sign of the cross, and while looking at them, I'd be somewhat fearful, feeling the judgment from the stony eyes looking back at me.

It was a modern Catholic church I went to with my friend, more of a new-wave version of the services I was used to going to as a child, and I found it refreshing. My friend also recommended a book on how to read the Bible, and once I finished that, I went out and bought a Bible for myself and started reading. It was research to me. I was trying to find an understanding of who God was and wondering if I could ever feel his presence around me.

One night as I sat on my couch, I was drunk and feeling alone and sorry for myself as I read my Bible. I read the words but felt nothing. It was just a story, like reading a novel. Frustrated, I stopped and asked God to come back into my life. I begged. *Please, God, if you are there, please let me know you are with me. Please, God, if you exist, let me know. Show me a sign—anything please!* It was probably the alcohol, but suddenly, I felt an overwhelming feeling of love and light and all-knowing sense that God existed and he was surrounding me. It was warm and inviting, just like I had hoped for.

I held the Bible against my chest and cried, a hard cry, rocking back and forth saying loudly, "Thank you! Thank you, God, for coming back to me. I know you are here. Thank you!" I stopped reading the Bible that night and never picked it up again; nor did I go back to church. But I did start praying every night. And I prayed every night the same prayer: *Please, God, please help me be peaceful and calm tomorrow. Help me get through the day without anger or depression. Help me find my happiness.* And I continued to talk with God often and ask a lot of questions. While I knew God was with me, I wasn't sure who he was or how I fit into his plan, and I needed answers.

As I searched to find my happiness, I still had demons deep inside me that needed resolving. I was only scraping the surface and needed to go further to find true happiness. My mind was calmer, more at ease, and no longer racing with thoughts of insecurity. I was more accepting of myself and confident to talk about my past. Yet as I cleared out my mind through yoga and meditation, I found myself aware that I was empty inside. That's when I found hypnotherapy. Hypnotherapy is a practice whereby you are hypnotized, and a therapist can tap into your subconscious to help you address things like smoking, post-traumatic stress disorder, or anxiety.

I never thought of doing hypnotherapy since I like to be in control, and the thought of someone tapping into my mind to take control made me nervous. However, my friend Kelly had recently become certified in hypnotherapy. I had met her through a mutual friend, and we connected immediately. We had a lot in common since she had an abusive past and was on her own spiritual and transformational journey. Our conversations centered around our pasts, our emotions, self-judgments, beliefs in God, seeing spirits, and past lives. I trusted her and asked her if she would treat me, not knowing if my subconscious could be broken into given that I had built this huge wall around me to shelter me from the world.

I was looking forward to my first session even though I wasn't sure I could be hypnotized. When I got there, we talked quite a bit about what my goals were with hypnotherapy and then talked about the process of how she would put me under. She told me that I would still be conscious and that we would explore the reasons why I was so depressed and sad all the time.

Kelly asked that I also write a healing journal to help with the process, and I've decided to include some of those entries in this book.

8/21 - I had my first hypnotherapy appointment today, and I was looking forward to it. I was in a place in my life where nothing had meaning for me. Not that it wasn't good. I have a very fortunate life, and I know it. I have a really good job that I like. It's challenging yet offers me a work-life balance that I need.

My kids are great. I only have them four days a week, and so I don't "lose it" as much as most moms I know. But they still get to me. I have rare moments of pure joy with them and other times mostly sadness.

My mom lives with me, and she does so much to help me and the boys. I do appreciate her, but she also annoys me. She has no other friends or interaction except with me, so she doesn't let me breathe when I am home.

I have so much, and yet I feel empty. I want to enjoy my life. I want to feel happiness and fortune every time I go home, not the feelings of resentment and responsibility that make me feel trapped.

I was asked beforehand to think about what it was that I wanted to heal. I knew what I wanted. I wanted to rid myself of the emptiness in me, the feeling I've had since I was a little girl. I thought it was from my abusive childhood. Sometime in my later years I realized it came from not just this life, but prior lives. The pain and turmoil I have been carrying through many lifetimes and was aware of since I was a child.

When I arrived, I knew it was a good sign when the parking meter had a paid ticket just sitting there, waiting for me. I'll take any good sign I can get.

Kelly, my friend, the hypnotherapist, looked so relaxed and comfortable in her role. She was glowing, and it just felt so right to be there. We talked about the emptiness and how I never felt happy. Soon after we began the session.

I went in there wholeheartedly. I *needed* it. My soul needed it. I knew I'd needed therapy for months. Therapy had worked for me before in my depressive states. That was when I lost my last pregnancy and when I left my husband. This time I had nothing to talk about—it was just that feeling of emptiness that has always been with me, and I wanted it gone. I was desperate. I needed to change my core, to fix that hole in my being, and I was ready.

Kelly started the session by having me visualize floating on a feather while she counted backward from 10.

I tried to picture my chocolate room where I had been practicing meditation, but I kept focusing on this meadow that Kelly was guiding me to. Long green grass up to three feet high. I want to land on it but not just on it, on *top* of it! I tried so hard, and when I finally landed on top of it, I was giddy like a schoolgirl. I kept it to myself since I knew I needed to focus on my friend and her questions.

She asked about the emptiness. The me on the feather got annoyed because she was leading me to some bad emotions. But I knew she was there to help me, so I trusted her. She asked a few more questions, and I began to answer them.

I felt as though I was awake with my eyes closed, and yet I couldn't control my answers. *Was I forcing them? Did I really feel them? Why am I saying these things?* The analytical me and the controlling me couldn't understand it was my subconscious mind speaking out loud to me.

Don't question. Don't think. Just go with it, I thought as I cried. I was crying because I knew the truth of what was coming felt familiar yet had been hidden inside me for so long.

We focused on the emptiness. I knew exactly where it was since it's been there my whole life. My friend asked me to give it a form so I could talk to it. It looked like a tube. A black tubular shape coming out of my side, with eyes. I talked to it. I asked it about the emptiness. I asked it what it needed to be fulfilled. And here's what I found it needed:

Happiness: To feel the pure joy and happiness I had felt the day before when I had a moment of it with my kids. We were out back, hanging out on the hammocks together, and it was there. A realization that in that moment I was so happy. That feeling was what I wanted more often. It was so fleeting. *Why couldn't I feel that all the time? Don't most people?*

That I am good enough: This one surprised me. I

always felt I was good at anything I put my mind to. And yet, deep inside, I felt I wasn't good enough.

Not for the next date.

Not for the new job.

Not for my kids. *That hurt!*

I know I'm a good parent, and yet I feel my kids don't deserve me. *Why?* I yell at them or get mad, and they still tell me I'm the most awesome mom ever! And instead of feeling elated, I walk away feeling like a lie to my own kids. I think, *they have no idea how fucked up I am, but they will see it when they are older. They will see that I am not good enough.*

It needs to know: The emptiness needs to know something. It needs to know about the past lives. The presences, feeling of people around me, whether they are real. *Are they real or is it all in my head?*

And lastly,

To serve God: *What? To serve God?* "So I can teach my kids to do so." Yup, that's what I said, and, boy, did I hesitate.

It took a long series of questions to get me to these conclusions, but these are what came out. I was surprised by my answers. When I was asked by my friend if all was fulfilled with the emptiness, I said yes.

I was still under hypnosis, and Kelly was starting to wake me up from my session when the strangest thing started to happen. Almost immediately, I felt this surge of electricity bolt through my arms. It started at my fingertips and shot right up through my arms and chest. I yelled, "What's happening?" I tried to listen to my friend and turned to her for answers. I didn't want to be scared.

She asked what I was feeling, and I said I saw a light pass my eyes, right to left, and then suddenly electricity so powerful it jolted me. It kept coursing through my arms, into my chest and up. Kelly said to trust it, so I did.

The lightning was strong. It came through me several times. It was preceded by a light flashing and by energy through my torso and up through my head. It was so powerful I thought, *She must be seeing this!* I started to breathe heavily. It was odd—I was conscious of it, and yet I had no control over it.

Being under hypnosis is weird in that while you are in it and experiencing it, your mind is a constant observer of it. I even thought to myself, almost jokingly, *Am I going to start speaking in tongues?*

As I had never been hypnotized, I assumed my friend knew what I was experiencing. I was waiting for her to tell me it was normal for this type of treatment. But she didn't. She told me her spiritual guides were telling her that it was a healing spirit and just to trust it. I gave in to the experience. I mean I *really needed this!* So, I would do and accept whatever came my way.

The electricity kept coming. At one point my body bucked up so hard since the jolt felt like a battery jumpstarting a car. And then the surges were smaller, and in between there was a coldness. A shivering that made me shudder.

The light was so bright, and yet it was not a light. Kelly asked me if it was the divine light, but I didn't understand, so I said no. It wasn't like a bulb shining in my face. And yet the entire sky, or ceiling (I had my eyes closed still), was so freaking white!

This amazing light was pushing me. Just pushing me down. And there was this aura around me, like a clear or cloudy circle surrounding me and pushing me. Pushing me so hard down into my chair. And then I became helpless as the energy took over. Kelly described it as a spiritual healing.

Suddenly I felt gray, so much gray, and it was me. This thing that was happening was pushing me so hard. And I could no longer move. It felt as though my body was three times its weight, and a force was pushing me into the chair. Then this energy began pulling at my limbs, going through my arms trying to pull the grayness out of me. I told my friend what was happening, and I flung my arms over the chair to the sides. This energy wanted out. It wanted to pull the grayness out of me. It was so much, so powerful, and so draining.

Waves of euphoria. Uncontrollable laughter like a high on drugs. Without hesitation, I asked her if I could laugh. I heard her laughing, and I laughed with her. I felt immense joy and laughter. I couldn't stop! I was euphoric, so I let it go as I knew laughter was healing. *I needed this, remember?*

I was physically drained and pleaded with this energy to stop. "Please stop. I can't take it anymore." "Please go. I'm so tired!"

Finally, I found enough strength to pull my arms back into the chair. My arms were tingling, and I'd lost feeling in my fingers. And then I wanted to sleep. I was tired, and slowly this thing released me as if it knew I couldn't handle it any longer. I assumed a fetal position in the chair and lay there in silence for a long time.

I asked Kelly to get me out of hypnosis. She started to talk to me, but I didn't hear what she said. Suddenly I was awake. I sat up, and my eyes opened, and I said, "I'm done."

I was thirsty and lightheaded. I drank a lot and tried to hydrate. I was so cold, and Kelly put two blankets on me. I tried to clear my head and drink. We talked about it, and after a while

I was OK.

My entire body ached like I had run a marathon. I was physically overwhelmed and beaten up! We talked, and I told her about my experiences. It was wonderful, and I felt so good. It took some time before I could go.

I was elated that I had made significant progress in only one session. Kelly was excited for me, and I knew I had to come back for more. But what happened in that session was only the start of what would continue later that night.

When I arrived home, over four hours had passed since I left my house for the session. My mom was anxiously awaiting me and wanted to know how it felt. I was tired and didn't want to talk about it, but she was asking me questions, so we sat down, and I told her all of it. She was concerned and asked if I had been given a drug beforehand. After talking with her, I sat down to watch some TV and to process what had happened. I knew I shouldn't be having alcohol, but I poured myself a glass of wine and drank anyway.

It was getting late, but I couldn't turn off. I finally went to bed and tossed and turned for a while until I finally fell asleep.

About an hour later I woke up with a startle. Something humanlike jumped on my bed and straddled me. I was sleeping on my stomach and felt a male presence. He was on his knees and drilling this energy force into my lower back.

I thought to myself, *Is this a dream?*—but only fleetingly since I knew it was real. This thing was strong and intrusive and yet it didn't feel negative. I tried to be accepting of it even though the unknown scared me a bit. While I thought through all this, the drilling continued and became more forceful. I couldn't move while this presence had me pinned. Then the pain started, and it was unbearable. It was in my lower back, where the energy was. I finally fought it. I pushed up with my arms as hard as I could and yelled out a primal scream, "AAAAAHHHHHHHH," getting higher and louder as I lifted my left shoulder and back until I could turn around.

And then I yelled, *"Stop it! Just stop it!"* And suddenly it was gone.

"Leave me alone!" I screamed. I pulled the covers over my head and began to pray to God. "Keep me safe, God. I don't understand, but please keep me safe".

I peeked over the covers a few times but saw nothing. My dog was barking nonstop. I got up to see what had excited him, but I saw nothing in the space he was barking at. He jumped into bed with me. I put my arm around his warm body, and I immediately passed out.

When I woke up the next morning, I felt a heightened sense of everything around me. Sounds, visions, lots of white images floating around me. I was so tired and yet so energized. I called Kelly before work to tell her what had happened. I needed an explanation. She said she would email her mentor and some colleagues but assured me that it was probably a good energy and that the healing spirits were continuing to do their job. She said to keep an open mind to whatever came my way since my spirit guides were with me, helping me.

Later that day, Kelly called to say that I had experienced a Kundalini awakening. "Kundalini" is a Sanskrit word meaning "coiled up." In Hinduism, it's related to the energy, known as a primal energy, that is built up at the base of one's spine. For most people, it lies dormant. In researching this the next few days, I realized that while many people have common experiences with it, it's only after years of intentional studying with healing or yoga masters that they can achieve it. Additionally, the symptoms or experiences I had during my session that day and in my bed that night were extremely rare. According to my friend and her mentor, I must have been really open to my spirit guides helping me. Her words brought me the comforting notion that someone was finally looking out for me.

That night another girlfriend of mine came over since she knew I'd had my session the night before. My mom was with us, and I began to tell them my story—not only of the session but also what had happened in bed. Immediately my friend asked me to pull up my shirt so she could look at my back. What she saw shocked the three of us. At the base of my spine was a large black and blue bruise, as if someone had hit me with a baseball bat.

Somewhat scared but also intrigued, I continued reading everything I could about Kundalini awakenings. I had to be careful, I read, as some people went mad from achieving Kundalini awakening, even after years of practice and wanting to release this energy. I went into the coming weeks with an open mind and forced myself not to be fearful of what may come. *It's just the universe speaking to me,* I thought. *Let it happen. It's all part of the process. Let it be. Just like in meditation, you are now an observer.*

8/28 - One week has passed, and the week has been a blur, but so many interesting insights and feelings have occurred. Here are some of the things I have been feeling/hearing this week:

Electricity surges. In my back, in my neck and in my arms. Very strong on day one but slowly subsiding.

Tingling in my legs to my groin. Feels like sparklers.

Increased sex drive! But no one to accept it!

Light flashes in my left eye. They are lingering and flowing and large.

Lots of white flowing images in my vision before I wake up and open my eyes in the morning.

Lights—red, many dots in moving formation. Which coincidentally matched images I saw in a video my friend sent me later that day!

Sounds, lots of them. Voices, but distant, a sense of not being alone. I hear music, beautiful music with sounds of mandolins and bells. I feel as though I'm hearing at a different vibrational level where no one else can.

Heightened senses. While lying in bed, I heard thumping and felt the bed moving, only to realize it was my blood flowing.

My energy affecting the lights around me. The front-porch lights went out as soon as I walked outside, all three of them, as I was waiting for a friend to pick me up for dinner. Lights flickered in the rooms I walked into.

I hate to say this for fear of it coming back, but the emptiness is gone. When I have those moments where it is usually there, I now have no feeling. Just acknowledgment that it's gone. So now what do I want that gap filled in with? You can't have pure joy when you're just sitting around alone, can you?

Kelly was sending me videos and email links to articles about Kundalini experiences, and as I viewed or read them, it was as if I was reading about myself. The visuals, the sounds, the electrical surges—all documented somewhere—exactly as I had experienced them! It was unreal. I was loving this new awareness in my life. And most importantly I was loving the fact that I was feeling better.

I continued to go to Kelly for my sessions. We worked through counseling and hypnotherapy, and each session exposed new healings and an understanding of myself and the pain. Our goal was to work on the four things I'd learned about myself in the first session. That I want happiness, that I have feelings of not being good enough, that I need to know about the spirits and whether they are real, and that I want to serve God. We worked on how I could overcome these obstacles and find my true purpose in life.

My sessions with Kelly would start with counseling as I caught her up on all the things going on in my life. We also talked about how the pain and fears I had experienced in my past were affecting my present life. Then we discussed what I wanted to work on in our hypnotherapy session. Once we agreed to a plan, Kelly would guide me through a visualization to get me into a hypnotized state.

I would picture myself floating on a large leaf in the sky and slowly falling until I landed on my favorite island. The island was gorgeous, with a beautiful sandy beach on the edge of an ocean, the place where I would meet with my healer and spirit guides.

As I stood on the beach, I could see someone from a distance waiting for me. I would walk up to a man dressed in a hooded black robe, and where his face should have been was nothing but light. He didn't speak, but we talked through telepathy.

"Welcome. I am your healer," he said. He gave me a big hug, filling me up with so much love. I trusted him instantly. Kelly prompted me to ask him questions to help me in my search for happiness, and he told me that he would offer what he could in guidance.

After he had no more answers for me, Kelly guided me to look around to see if there was anything significant that I should notice. There was a path that led into the forest. I asked him if I should follow the path, and he replied without words, "Yes, follow me." After a short walk in, I saw a clearing in the woods with a structure made of stone that looked like an old temple. In front of the temple was a large circle of rocks, and standing around the rocks stood these beings. Each one was a beam of light, vaguely humanlike in form, with no discerning features or faces. My healer told me they were my spirit guides. As I walked toward them, they surrounded me with their light and welcomed me with the most joyous of emotions. As I entered their circle, I became one with them and felt at home.

It became a ritual to meet with them during each hypnotherapy session. Sometimes we would circle in flight high into the sky where I would giggle with laughter. Sometimes after the welcoming, one of the beings of light would take my hand and lead me to a beautiful lake amid tall, colorful trees. We walked together, swam together, and enjoyed the waterfall. We spoke only through our emotions. And after each parting they would remind me that they were always with me, even when I was not under hypnosis.

After some time under hypnosis, I would find that Kelly would at first try to guide me during the sessions, but my mind was always ahead of her, and I would go my own way. I'd let her know and fill her in on what was going on whenever I could. And when my time was up, I would just wake up. It was rare for people to wake up out of hypnosis on their own, but I always did. I never needed guiding out of hypnosis since my healers and I always knew when it was time to end our assemblies.

These experiences in hypnotherapy and meditation strengthened my spiritual beliefs. I believed in God and guardian angels and found comfort in having guides around me. I was no longer alone.

Today my healer and spirit guides are always with me, and I can see their light when I call to them, asking for their guidance. I'm grateful to have met them and glad that they continue to surround me with their love and presence.

I continued meditation at home and journaled often since it helped me clear my thoughts. I found when I put my thoughts on paper, I was honest with myself and my emotions. These practices brought me peace and a greater understanding of who I really was. It also made me more aware of my ups and downs. As I would go back in time and read pages of weeks prior, I could see that I still had a long way to recovery.

10/11 - I haven't written in weeks. I'm back from a trip to Fiji, and it was a very emotional trip. I felt very connected emotionally with the island, the people, and the women there. My friend said I was exuding a strong female energy since I had some great moments with the women on the island.

I cried about missing the kids and fell apart after calling them. I was so weak, and maybe it was the spirit of the island. Being there with the people and the poverty in the villages was very moving and made me put things into perspective.

Back only a few days, and the stress returns. And yet I love being with my kids and seeing them again. They have grown, and they are so adorable and loving. I love them and feel more connected to them.

Another session coming up, and I hope it goes well. I fear my validation may be invalidated? We'll see. I'm still striving so hard for peace. It will come one day.

12/1 - I just came from a session, and it was so good and enlightening. I don't know how to describe what I'm going through. I don't know how to explain it, but these sessions are so helpful, and I feel great. I'm happy. I enjoy my time with my kids. More importantly, I am closer to God and my reasons for being here in this life. I know I am being looked over, watched, protected. I am generally happy and have purpose. Things make sense, and I know it will be OK. And I am healing from my past. It's all I can ask for.

12/16 – Stress, expectations, time. Too much of the first two and not enough of the last. A formula for disaster. Expectations—too many. Too many responsibilities for others, and I think about moving far away, and yet I'm torn. Guilty if I go, leaving everyone behind.

Tonight, I yelled at the kids, my mom, the dogs. It was unjustified. I'm sad and ashamed as they did not deserve my anger. I hate this, hate how I get here, just tired of the holidays and all the work. I want to please, I need to do, and yet what's in it for me? I'm tired, irritated, broken, angry, and sad. How can I simplify without letting others down? I can't. I suck it up while it sucks up my energy.

I don't like the hard times. I'm tired of them, and they bring out the worst in me. In thoughts, in sadness, in my reaction to my kids. I want to be good all the time. How will they rate me? How will they sum me up in one sentence when they are older? I hope it's good. I love them so much and just want to protect them.

I was struggling. I knew I was getting better, but I was still an emotional wreck, still questioning myself as I continued to go from extremely sad to extremely happy—sometimes all in one day. The peace I felt in those moments of joy was incredible. But then something would happen, and I'd sink back to sadness and depression.

I continued with my sessions. Each one brought me the validation, joy, and peace that I was looking for. Each one motivated me to continue with yoga, meditating, and praying to God each night. I knew it was working, but I still had a long road ahead of me. And when I doubted if I could continue in my commitment to heal, I reminded myself of my new mantra: *Every cloud is followed by sunshine, darkness always comes before the dawn, and similar to a scab that looks worse while it's healing, be patient and trust the process.*

As I continued to struggle, Kelly recommended that I try hypnosis for post-traumatic stress disorder (PTSD) therapy. In this therapy we would regress back to a time when my father was abusive. She said we could "recreate my memories" to heal my emotions regarding my father. I was trusting the process and was willing to try anything she recommended since I was seeing results.

As Kelly brought me under hypnosis, instead of taking me to my favorite island, this time she took me to a large movie theater and asked me to take a seat. It was empty except for me and a large movie screen in front of me with the curtains closed. As I sat down, she asked me to remember an experience from when I was a child with my dad. When the curtains opened, it was as if I was watching a live play of myself as a child on the stage in front of me.

I watched myself sitting at the dinner table with my dad as he yelled at me for not eating. I ran up the stairs to my bedroom as he hit me with his belt. Then he beat me while I hid under the covers. Then the movie ended with me praying to God that my dad die in his sleep.

I was angry and hurt and felt unloved. Kelly rewound the film and played it back again; only this time she asked me how I would have liked the movie to have played out. Instead of my dad beating me up, this time he put me on his lap and told me he loved me. He had empathy for my stomach hurting. He hugged me and told me that all would be OK. Kelly rewound the film yet again, and we played it back, making small changes until I was satisfied with my movie.

When I awoke, something had changed in me. I felt different. I felt loved.

Over the next few weeks, after that session, I kept trying to see if I could find that familiar feeling inside me of not being loved. But it was gone. Thinking about my past with my dad no longer brought me sadness or anger. I didn't forget the original story of my dad and his beating, but the emotions behind that experience had changed to match that of the new movie I had created.

I did a few more sessions of PTSD therapy to go back and recreate my experiences with my ex-husband and one session to recreate an episode with my kids to overcome the guilt I had from bullying them the night my son threw up and when I had a meltdown while my kids stood by watching me and crying. Each session relieved me of my guilt associated with my actions and anger at those around me, and it brought comfort that I was succeeding in "fixing myself at the core, from the inside out."

1/22 - I'm stuck. What is my purpose? I know I need to be here for my kids—they need me. But the facade that is my life doesn't seem real. I'm playing a role I don't have the script for.

I'm no longer depressed, just weighed down with the overwhelming responsibilities of everyone wanting something of me always. Who am I? When I'm in session or in meditation, I feel normal, validated, comfortable in my own skin, and at peace. Then I'm unaided and think once again that I'm crazy and not normal. Scared, uneasy, hating where I am. Why?

And so it went. Joy, sadness, and more joy. Pure love and compassion one day, frustration the next. And yet growth—my mind had expanded and my beliefs blown apart.

My relationship with my kids was getting better, and that was the most important thing to me. One day we were at home playing video games, and then we started dancing to music. My son Tino looked over at me, almost through me, with a huge smile on his face. He was so happy, and I knew deep down he was happy because he was watching his mom laughing and having fun. That gave me the encouragement to continue my path to find myself and fix my brokenness. I wanted my boys to see their mom as a happy person, not as the detached, sad, depressed, crying woman they had been exposed to most of their lives. I was unhappy, and they knew it, but that day they saw a glimmer of hope, and I knew I had to do it not only for myself but for them.

I continued the hypnotherapy and counseling sessions since they were helping me. The sessions were amazing, and those continued to supplement my home meditation practice. In each one I learned more about myself and who I truly was.

The first time I regressed into a past life during hypnotherapy, it was unplanned. I was entering a healing session when suddenly my body began to jolt while waves of electricity surged through me. The smell of incense burning permeated my nose as I walked through cavernous walls until I came into a dungeon where I was being held captive. As the story unfolded, I learned I was the daughter of a wealthy leader of Greek descent. The year was sometime around 600 BC. I was being held because of my lineage, and I had been raped multiple times during my captivity.

Eventually released, I found myself standing at the edge of a lake. I was wearing a white robe, and I had long dark hair. I was admiring the beauty of the landscape. Suddenly, I felt a stabbing pain in my back as a large knife entered my back twice. Then I was pushed into the water. I screamed out, feeling physical pain while lying in the chair of Kelly's office, caught between the consciousness of my present and past life. I realized it was my brother who had murdered me.

I sank into the water, suffocating, dying, until I suddenly felt an overwhelming presence enveloping my entire body. I felt safe though I was not sure what was happening. I tunneled through the water as if flying, being carried by someone, and it seemed like forever until we stopped. When I looked at my surroundings, I was standing in what looked like a bus depot. Many people, all wearing white, their bodies transparent in nature, were hustling about as if we were at Union Station in New York City. A group of them formed a circle around me, welcoming me, though no one said a word.

Then I stood in line until I was led into an empty room. It was white like everything else. The only thing I saw was a cot and a man in front of me holding a drink. We spoke telepathically, and I acknowledged my death and drank his elixir. This drink, I was told, was to cleanse me of the life I'd just lived and to prepare me for going back to earth for my next one. Then I was prompted to lie down on the cot and close my eyes. With that, I awoke from my healing session.

I was exhilarated! I couldn't believe what had just happened. I spent the next few weeks trying to process it. There was a calmness in me that I hadn't had before. I realized I wasn't as fearful as I had been in the past, and a few months later, when I was on a beach trip with a girlfriend, I realized I was no longer fearful of the ocean—as I once had been. I had been to the beach many times, and I absolutely loved the beach, but the deep water had always terrified me. I enjoyed the ocean and went in, but I never swam through it, never completely submerged myself in its waters. I was so afraid of the deep that even walking into an aquarium would send panic into my veins.

On this trip, however, I swam underwater and never even thought about the fear until I realized it wasn't there. While I can still be intimidated by the large vastness of an ocean, and of course the occasional thought of being eaten by a shark, my former overwhelming panic is gone.

I continued to keep an open mind with these experiences. When I told a girlfriend of mine what had been happening, she gave me a book called *Many Lives, Many Masters* by Brian L. Weiss. It's about a woman who, like me, had experiences of past lives through hypnosis. That book really resonated with me. The woman's stories reminded me of my nightmares as a child, which, throughout the years, I came to believe were me in some sort of past life. This book, along with my recent experiences under hypnosis, made me certain that they were.

What was happening was real to me, and anytime I started to question the process, I would question my sanity. I had to believe because, for one, if I didn't, my only other choice was that I was nuts. But most importantly, it was working, and my fears were dissolving. I had several more experiences with past lives and between lives during these sessions; most of them were unplanned and occurring shortly after going under hypnosis.

In one session as I was going under, I started feeling extreme pain around my midsection. I cried out in pain. Suddenly, I found myself in the body of a soldier in the middle of a large land area, surrounded by dead men who had lost their lives in battle. The lower half of my body was missing. This soldier reminded me of my earlier nightmares as a child.

In another, I was a young girl living in the mountains with her brother and father. There was a fight and rage, and both my brother and I were killed by our father with a large boulder to each of our heads.

Each death ended at the bus depot, with me drinking the cleansing elixir and readying myself for another adventure on this earth. In some hypnotherapy sessions, I would go right into a between life in the bus depot getting ready for the next life. With each life and cleansing, my fears were dissolving, and I was learning more about my true self.

In my first session under hypnosis, I had told Kelly that I wanted to find happiness, that I felt I wasn't good enough, and that I needed to know if the spirits around me and my dreams of past lives were real. All of those questions were resolving themselves with this therapy, and it was changing me, changing the core of who I was. I continued to work outside of therapy with my meditation practice, with yoga, and with reading anything I could find to assist me on my self-help journey. The only thing still remaining was my request to serve God.

Many times driving to my hypnotherapy sessions I would feel a throbbing in my brain, around my forehead—or what some call the third eye (a Hindu and Buddhist expression describing wisdom in the forehead, or the gate into a higher consciousness).

As I got closer to her office, the throbbing would become almost unbearable. On those days, once I was under hypnosis, I would begin my healing journey, and my focus would be distracted by this throbbing. And my third eye would strain as it transformed into a door with the most beautiful blue or purple light bursting through the seams, wanting the door to be opened. As I concentrated, the throbbing would deepen, the door would fly open, and everything would go black. I would feel my eyes darting back and forth furiously, and I would know the masters were coming.

I didn't know who the masters were, but waiting for them brought me excitement and uncertainty. *What do they want me to see today?* They were there with me. I felt them surround me as if they were a congregation of intelligence, yet I couldn't see them. Sometimes they arrived showing me quick flashes of pictures with unfamiliar faces and objects, my past in this life, my past in other lives, the future, and some things I didn't understand.

They didn't speak, and yet they did. I asked questions, sometimes prompted by my hypnotherapist, about things I wanted to learn about myself and sometimes about the visions they showed me. They were the masters, the elders, they told me, and they wanted me to know there was more to this life than meets the eye. I learned about the universe and how we are all connected, one energy, one source, all of us.

My beliefs of knowing one God changed to an understanding that we are all God. Their messages were unreal, something new to me, but I knew they were teaching me, so I listened and observed. I felt blessed by their holy presence—full of knowledge—and they wanted to share with me. And when they were done, I would wake up and return to consciousness, trying to make sense of this third-eye explosion, like a downloading of information that they had provided me.

While they only spoke to me during these times, they told me they were always around me, and I could call to them whenever I needed reassurance. And when I do, they don't talk back like they do in my sessions, but they provide me signs when I ask them. When the universe speaks to me as trees wave on my command, I know it's the masters. When I notice the plants are alive and have consciousness, I know it's the masters showing me where I come from. And through the masters I know my home is the universe—the spiritual world that extends far beyond this physical earth.

One night I was standing outside, looking up at the sky, and I asked for a sign that they heard my plea for guidance. Almost immediately something dropped from the sky, hit the floor in front of me, and bounced a few feet away. I walked over to it and saw that it was a dead mouse. I'm sure it was dropped by an owl that lived near my house, and yet it was the assurance I needed that the masters were real and that they had heard my plea.

One of my dogs Rex, is a nine-year-old golden retriever-spaniel mix, and he's adorable. When I rescued him, he was about a year old and was growling at everyone who passed by him but me. I had been looking for a companion for my older lab for about a year—not seriously, but I'd kept my eye out for another dog and figured when I saw the right one, I would know it.

When I went to the pet store that day, I didn't realize they were having rescue adoptions. As I walked into the store and passed by Rex on the sidewalk, I did a double take; then I stopped to pet him. I went into the store to pick up whatever items I needed, but Rex was on my mind the entire time. Before I left, I told the woman I had to go pick up my kids but that I was coming back to get him.

That day Rex came home with us. I knew right from the start that he was special. I took him on walks with me every day, but I soon found that Rex couldn't keep up. He'd sit down twenty minutes into our walk and not want to get up. I thought it was because he was a recent rescue and probably needed to be healthier. He had gotten a checkup and a clean bill of health except for mites. He'd had hundreds of them on him, which I hadn't noticed. The mites took weeks to clear, and while I continued to walk Rex, he still would tire easily.

After several months I took him in again, and he tested positive for heartworms. He needed to go through a cure treatment, which was risky. He had to have several shots of what was basically arsenic over several weeks and then spend months in a crate so we could limit his movement. During this time, I had ruptured my Achilles tendon and needed surgery. Just before my surgery, I went to a hypnotherapy appointment and asked for a healing session. I had told Kelly about Rex and that I was concerned for his health too.

While in session, Kelly had me envision a white, healing light surrounding me and then flowing through me until it exploded through the ceiling into the skies. Once I reached that place, she did something that surprised me. She called Rex into our session. Rex came bounding out of the sky and into my vision as he always did at home. Whenever I came home, Rex would come out from wherever he was and jump all over me, showering me with love. He would follow me around the house, jumping on me with excitement until he settled down.

In this session he came in the same way, only once he got closer and jumped on me, he was bigger than ever, just glowing with a beautiful golden-and-white light. He put his paws on my shoulders (he's not tall enough to do that in real life) and just smiled—a smile so big it made me laugh. He then hugged me with his body and light and picked me up, spinning us up into the sky. We were one, and during this time he told me he was my spirit guide, and we would forever be linked through our souls. I was filled with so much joy and happiness. He told me that we were both going to be OK. In response, I said to him, "Rex, if you are really here, please, when I get home tonight, don't jump on me. Just sit in front of me and let me know that you were really here with me today."

After the session I went home. I couldn't wait to see Rex. As I walked in the door, there he was, quietly sitting and looking at me. I was floored! He sat patiently as I bent down to hug him and put my head on his. I looked into his eyes and I knew—we both knew—what had happened was real. I thanked him for joining me in my session and for being my spirit guide. He never jumped on me that night. I still couldn't believe it, and as I walked into the kitchen toward the stairs to go to my bedroom, he ran in front of me and then just sat there, looking at me. He did it several times, and I got chills. I told him repeatedly, "I understand, Rex. I know you were there. Thank you for letting me know!"

We both recovered, and he and I have had a different relationship ever since. Every morning when I leave the house, I look for Rex and give him a big hug and ask him to watch over everyone. I also ask him for guidance. He is my living spirit guide, and he brings me comfort. He is a reminder that I'm being looked after.

Sometimes when I meditate, he joins me. One day when I was meditating alone in my room, I felt this intense urge to smile. I couldn't explain it, but I was being prompted by someone or something to smile. With eyes closed, I did, and inside I was glowing. When I finally opened my eyes, there was Rex, lying on a pillow near me, with his eyes closed and a big smile on his face. I couldn't resist snapping a photo of him.

Years later, my sons and I went to an animal psychic, and we showed her photos of our dogs. Without having been told anything, she immediately called out Rex and said that he was very special and that he looked out for all of us and would be with us for a long time.

ALL OF THE WORK THAT I was doing with hypnotherapy, yoga, meditation, my research, and speaking to God was working. I was starting to let go of attachments that I had to fears and negative emotions, and as I continued my practices, I continued to see improvement.

The experiences I had during hypnotherapy may not be common, but they do occur for some. I did not go searching for any of these—I was looking to find peace and happiness in my life. As I did so, I continued with my meditation practices and speaking to God, my healer, my spirit guides, and the masters while I found my faith again.

During my sessions and meditations, I have met God and Jesus Christ and my higher self. I have had the most incredible experiences on the other side of this universe. I've met my healer and all the wonderful guides, masters, and mentors that helped me understand and that truly know me.

My spirit guides are always with me, and I know them well—I've met them. I tried to maintain my healing journal, but I couldn't keep up with my experiences. Every day seemed a miracle in itself, and there was so much information, and all of it was too difficult to put into words. It didn't matter; I was living it and learning from each session. The memories of these sessions are waning, but the lessons will remain forever. I have read books that validated what I experienced, which gave me confidence to speak about them without fear. I started sleeping better, and the nightmares became dreams of healing. I was no longer fearful of the night.

Once my mind was at peace, alcohol was no longer a problem for me. I cut back on my drinking significantly since I no longer needed it to escape. People talk about their addictions around drugs and alcohol, and many times they look for cures for their dependency without resolving the real issues that are driving those behaviors. For me, using was a way to escape myself and my circumstances, and once my need to escape was gone, so was my need to consume those things.

Two years after my commitment, I stood looking in the mirror at my naked self and I had a revelation. I had achieved the goal of my tattoo. I was the lotus flower that bloomed. My heart was surrounded by the love of God, my spirit guides, my healer, and the masters. *Amazing,* I told myself. *I did it.*

I was finally happy. I continued counseling and hypnotherapy for five years, until I no longer needed them. I've learned to live without fears, guilt, or regrets. I worked on all sorts of issues in the beginning, and then when I had exhausted all my demons, I focused on what I called maintenance. Then at some point, Kelly and I decided it was time to end the sessions. People come and go in your life. Kelly and I are no longer connected. We always knew we were brought together so we could help each other. Kelly grew personally and learned as much during my sessions as I did. She came into my life to heal me and learn with me, and that must have been our agreement before we came to this earth.

During my transformation I was also introduced to a wonderful man, Mike. I met him on a blind date, and he is now my husband. Mike was on a similar path of transformation when we met, and now we continue our journey together with our blended family of four children. Our relationship is built upon respect and friendship. We inspire each other and are very supportive of each other. We are always teaching and learning from each other. Our life is simple—it revolves around walking, exploring, reading, watching TV, and spending time with our family and dogs.

In my journey to heal, I learned to forgive and love myself and others. I also learned patience and how to deal with my emotions. I still get angry, sad, and depressed. But I've learned to accept that those emotions are OK—it's how you deal with them that's important. And more importantly, the emotions are no longer driven by my victim curse. In the past, on a scale of one to ten, my lowest emotion was below a one, and at my happiest I was at a five. These days, my lows are a five, and my highs are ten, with most days being somewhere closer to ten.

I've learned that life is hard, and bad things happen, but there is also a lot of good in the world and in my life. I see the positive things in life. I am an optimist now, always looking for the silver lining. I am Job. My sister the Princess once told me that no matter what happens in my life, no matter how difficult it becomes, I always come up smelling like roses. It took me a long time to believe that, and now I get it. We all have silver linings. We all smell like roses.

AN ENLIGHTENMENT EXPERIENCE

I have always looked at life through dissatisfied eyes, never sure of the things that they focus on.

I wonder if there is more—more than the simple charade game that everyone around me seems to be playing.

Omniscience seems impossible to me, although unconsciously I find myself striving for it each day.

On my way home from another ordinary day of work, taking in my day's experiences and knowing tomorrow will be the same, I notice the beautiful sunset over the horizon.

As many ultimate questions race through my mind, I feel an urge to view that sunset and find the answers.

Standing high on a mountain, I see my first unobstructed view. Upon this first sight I see a large bright orange circle, and within that circle is a small yellow spot. This yellow spot acts as a controller, as if it were the sun's main source of being.

Surrounding this huge circle, I see more orange, which is then outlined by a deep blue. Spread out for miles over the sky, this sunset seems to be watching the world that stands beneath me. The only word describing this sight at this moment is "amazing."

My mind runs faster as I enter into a state of non-ordinary reality. I feel a sudden rush of blood in my veins, and everything in my field of vision, and beyond, seems to be in focus.

For the first time in my life, omniscience doesn't seem impossible, and I now sit back with a feeling of satisfaction, knowing there is so much more to experience in my life, and that all I have is time to enjoy those experiences.

When I was in high school, I had to write a paper based off an actual experience, and I wrote about my hopes for a future. "An Enlightenment Experience" was my paper.

I've had a lot of successes along with challenges since I wrote that paper, and yet I notice a similarity to my mind-set and where I am today. I was struggling back then, but I was still so hopeful of a bright future and ready for what life might bring my way. Over the years, however, I couldn't maintain that optimism, and my life spiraled out of control. Every year and every decade brought more pain and hurt, and I struggled to maintain my sanity.

Today I'm hopeful yet again, and I look forward to a future without the internal struggle of my own suffering. My husband, Mike, always quotes Haruki Murakami: "Pain is inevitable. Suffering is optional." I choose to move forward without the suffering.

I continue to work on myself. I work on having more compassion—real, pure, on-the-Dalai-Lama-scale compassion. I make judgments about people at times, but I work to avoid that. I struggle as a parent to give my kids the freedom they need to write their own script while still trying to force them within mine—as many parents do—but I work to maintain a proper balance. The difference is that I'm having fun doing the work, and I look forward to the future, whatever it may become.

I am enjoying my life. I enjoy my career and still want to challenge myself and grow in that area. I'm writing this book, and I am going to get it published. I want to buy land with my husband, teach workshops, and hold retreats there. I want to speak on a TED Talk. I want to buy an RV and travel the states. I want to get on a plane and travel the world. Most importantly, I want to share my story and let everyone know that I am in their circle and that they are not alone.

I have things to do, places to go, and people to see. My life is simple, mundane, busy, sometimes stressful, challenging, and exhausting. It's also exciting, peaceful, positive, loving, and hopeful, and I have a lot to look forward to. I have transformed, and finally I'm happy. Most importantly, I love myself, and to quote a song made famous by Timbuk 3: "The future's so bright, I gotta wear shades"!

4

MINDFUL SHIFTS

DURING MY TRANSFORMATION, I needed to put aside all the beliefs I had about myself and my past in order to heal. I reminded myself to keep an open mind about what I was learning. It was necessary for me to break free of the negative thinking and change my perspective of my life. It was that open mind that helped me change my thinking and behaviors of the previous decades and allowed me to move forward to find love for myself and those around me.

These days I find myself wanting to share my experiences with my friends and colleagues whenever the moment strikes me, usually when they are complimenting me on my optimism or sharing a personal story looking for guidance when, unknown to them, I may have experienced the same thing they are going through. I have learned that my experiences are not my own since many have gone through what I have. And I have learned that my courage to share them with others has had a profound effect on those that I share them with. In our moments of sharing, I see their appearances change, their faces relax as they realize they are not alone and no longer have to hide behind masks of perfection.

Throughout my healing journey, I learned to take my experiences and life's lessons and adjust my thinking to how I approached challenges. This change in thinking I refer to as Mindful Shifts.

FORGIVENESS—Before my transformation, and after eighteen years of not speaking to my father, I was convinced by my oldest sister, Rosetta, to go see him. She was the only one who spoke with him at the time since the rest of us had broken contact with him after my parents' divorce. Rosetta told me he'd changed, that he had a lot of regrets in his life, and that he missed his children. Although I still feared him, I agreed to see him if she met me there.

I drove to his house and rang the doorbell, knowing he and my sister were waiting for me inside. As he opened the door, he stood there crying, overwhelmed with the joy of seeing his daughter after so many years. In front of me I saw a frail, old man. He had aged quite a bit. I walked up to him and gave him a hug, but I felt nothing for this man.

I walked inside, and we talked for about an hour. I was detached. I kept my walls up. I felt sorry for him, this man I no longer knew. After that visit we spoke on the phone a few times a year, as I appeased him while meeting my obligation to him as a daughter. I would listen mostly and then hang up, glad the call was over. I used to hate my father, and over the years I'd cursed him countless times in loud, angry fights with him when I was alone. I wished him dead since I thought I would feel better once he died and that only in his death would my anger go away. After my visit I no longer wished he was dead, but while the anger had gone, those feelings had not been replaced by love.

I visited him once more to introduce him to my sons. He was delighted to see my kids and was very loving toward them. He sat them on his lap and smiled. It was painful for me to see that, as it reminded me of my childhood, sitting on his lap and longing to feel love from him.

It wasn't until I was going through my divorce, that we really reconnected. I called my father to tell him, and his reaction startled me. He cried. All four of his kids were divorced at that point, and he blamed himself. He said that if he hadn't cheated on my mom and gotten divorced, we wouldn't have all done the same. My dad also told me that he thought the reason I hadn't spoken to him for so many years was because I was siding with my mom in their divorce. He was showing me his vulnerability, a side of him I rarely saw, which allowed me to open up to him about the abuse.

"I didn't not speak with you because of the divorce," I told him. "I stopped talking to you because you hit me all the time. I was angry at you, and I couldn't be around you anymore." My dad was surprised to hear my reason for our estrangement.

"Marisa, I did the best I could as a father. I worked hard to provide for you and the family. It was hard for me as a father to see you doing drugs and going out all night and not coming home for days. I always worried about you, and I didn't know how to be a better father. I learned from how my parents raised me."

He had tried his best to provide for our family and had struggled with being an immigrant in America and trying to make a life for himself and his family. He knew he was making mistakes, and it only got worse when I started fighting back, sneaking out of the house, and using drugs. His story was honest, and it portrayed an innocence I had never seen from my dad. We talked for an hour about the past and our emotions, how we both felt betrayed, and together we cried. Neither one of us apologized on that call, and I realized then that neither one of us was right or wrong; it just was.

Before we hung up, I said, "I love you," and he responded, "I love you too, Marisa." I forgave my dad that day, and the empty space that my departed anger for him had left behind was once again filled back up—this time with love.

Over the last ten years, he and I have gotten much closer, and we talk a few times a month now. I have visited him in person and even stayed at his house. My dad is struggling with his own demons still. He suffers from depression due to regret, guilt, and loneliness. He is eighty-six and harmless, but he can still have violent tendencies. He has not shown me those directly, but toward others he has, so I am cautious. Still, he can be very gentle and kind and is a very loving father and grandfather. We have great talks on all kinds of topics, and I enjoy our conversations.

I've also have forgiven my ex-husband, as I've learned that I was part of the problem in our relationship. We were young when we met, and neither one of us knew how to be truly present in a relationship. Our relationship is now amicable, and we are very supportive of each other's spouses when coparenting our children together.

My practice of meditation was significant in finding this forgiveness. In the past I blamed God for my suffering and my relationship with my dad, but now I believe that my dad and I had an agreement long before either of us were born on this earth to teach and learn from each other. We have accomplished what we came here to learn together.

Not everyone can get to forgiveness, and some acts toward a human being are so atrocious that they would be hard to forgive. But forgiveness can start just by having compassion toward one another in the most simplistic settings.

When I was going through my infertility issues, the sight of a pregnant woman or baby would throw me into a state of anger. I remember standing in line at the grocery store, and a woman had a baby in the shopping cart in front of me. This baby was right next to me, trying to get my attention, and the woman was so proud of her young child and said something to me. I can't recall my response, but I do remember that I reacted negatively toward her and her child and said something mean. My reaction to her had nothing to do with her—it was my own self-pity that led me to lash out at her.

I try to remember that incident when I have an interaction with someone who reacts negatively to me. If a cashier is being nasty to me while I'm at a register, I try to think of what that person might be going through to prompt that behavior. Does the person have a sick child? Is the person alone or unable to pay the rent? Maybe the person is in an abusive relationship? Maybe being a mean-spirited person is just part of a persona. Maybe the person is a victim of a self-inflicted curse. Whatever this other person is going through, it's not about me. It's easy to react in these situations, but I try to have compassion and not have it affect me for the rest of the day. In Don Miguel Ruiz's book *The Four Agreements*, he discusses this topic in a chapter called "Don't Take Anything Personally." He stresses the point that the way other people react to you is not always about you.

After my divorce, I met a woman who owned a restaurant I frequented. I would sit at her bar drinking while the restaurant opened, and once it closed for the evening we'd head out to the bars. We became close friends and even took a few vacations together. However, we fought a lot since she often would speak to me disrespectfully.

On one occasion, we were traveling together, and I wanted to get to the airport two hours early. She fought me on this since she wanted to wait until the last minute to leave. I had traveled a lot for work, so it wasn't like I was new to travel. She caved to my request, and as we sat at the airport gate, she berated me for being so early. Then she literally said to me, "Go sit at that table over there away from me. I don't even want to see you or speak to you." Can you imagine a grown woman talking to me, her friend, as if I were a child? Not that you'd want to speak that way to a child. There were many times she treated me that way, and ultimately, I knew it was time for us to part ways.

I have no ill will toward my friend. As an adult woman she has her own demons, created when her father treated her badly when she was young. I choose not to be around her. Forgiveness doesn't mean that you need to include someone in your life if that person has mistreated you. If someone in your life is toxic, you can forgive the person without having to continue your connection with that person. Forgiveness is about showing compassion and sending love to individuals so they can overcome whatever is causing them to behave in a negative way, even if the compassion and love you send them are from a distance.

Most importantly, forgive yourself. When my kids were young, I felt guilt over how I was raising them. It was a difficult time in my life, and I didn't always feel I was the best mom. In my hypnotherapy sessions, I learned that I didn't ever feel "good enough" for any of the roles I played in my life, but those times are gone. Through my healing sessions, I learned to accept and love myself for exactly who I am. And with God by my side, I learned to forgive myself over my actions and decisions and ask guidance to be a better person.

If I hadn't forgiven myself, I would have continued to live in guilt and regret, which would have done no one any good. If I was guilty and had regret over how I raised my kids, then my energy would be consumed with the past instead of directed toward moving forward. Those feelings will not change my kids' past. So I forgave myself for those times, and I now work on having a better relationship with my kids in the present and for the future.

We go through life beating ourselves up for every thought we have, decision we make, or action we do. We hide our true selves in front of peers so we can "fit in." We choose to take paths that are uncomfortable for us because we are afraid to hurt those around us or we want to avoid judgment from others. Be truthful and kind to yourself in how you live your life, and make decisions based on what makes you happy. If your intentions are born from loving kindness, no one will get hurt, and you will not be judged.

Being truthful and forgiving toward yourself will relieve you of many physical ills and mental anguish. What you think is exactly what you think. What you feel is exactly what you feel. Accept it as your truth and work toward changing the negative thoughts and feelings to more positive ones. If you want to change these thoughts or feelings, there are ways to work on doing it.

One of the first things you need to do, however, is forgive yourself. Accept your thoughts, accept your decisions and actions, and honor yourself by not feeling guilt or regret about them. It's OK not to love someone or something, or a situation, but don't continue to bear the burden of your thoughts. Learn to forgive yourself for who you are and where you came from. Love and accept your past, even if your emotions are embroiled in something that happened as recently as the day before. Forgive your thoughts and feelings. It's OK to be you.

EXPECTATIONS—My husband, Mike, often jokes about wanting his own bedroom, and in the past we used to get into heated arguments about it. When we first moved in together, he moved into the house I shared with my mom and kids. He wanted to keep his apartment so he would have a place to spend time alone and also sleep.

Mike had two young daughters and wanted us to be a family, but having his own place meant he still kept his independence. I argued the notion that a family lives together, and one partner doesn't keep an apartment on the side. While he didn't keep the apartment, to this day he still wants his own bedroom and brings it up from time to time. Mike, at six feet four inches, just wants to sleep comfortably, and he enjoys watching TV before bed. I'm much smaller and like to sleep with the TV off, so when it's time for me to fall asleep, he compromises and turns down the volume. But with him, me, and a couple of dogs sleeping together, our bed can get pretty crowded.

I came into the relationship with expectations that a couple should sleep together because if we didn't, we would lose our connection and closeness that I had enjoyed in the evenings in one bed. My husband's was to just sleep comfortably, and he felt that we could still remain close even from separate bedrooms. After more than seven years, it's an argument that we continue to have regularly, but it no longer includes the heated exchanges of the past.

In almost any situation we put ourselves in, we bring to it our own set of expectations. Whether it's walking into the grocery store for ice cream, going into a meeting at work, or moving in with a new spouse, we unknowingly walk into it with a set of rules we have created based on past experiences.

When I was going through my infertility period, I had expectations that once I wanted a baby I would automatically get pregnant. And then once I did get pregnant, I had expectations that I would carry that baby through full-term. Because my expectations were not met during those times, I spent ten years of my life in a sad and depressed state. Each month in the beginning, I expected a positive pregnancy test, and then the situation changed, and each month I expected a negative test since it had always turned out that way. My expectations that I should carry a child had consumed me and made me a victim, and that thinking contributed to staying within my own prison with the curse I had placed upon myself. It wasn't until I changed my expectations and realized that I could adopt my second child that I started feeling better about my situation.

A few years ago, I lost my job. My initial expectation was to find another job soon after. When it didn't happen right away, I started to sulk and get depressed. My husband convinced me that I needed to let go of my attachment to finding the perfect nine-to-five job and spend the summer with him and our kids. I had gotten a severance check to cover expenses for a few months, but my expectation of going back to work to keep the money flowing kept gnawing at me. I had attached myself to what I thought would make me happy.

But I took his advice. I practiced yoga, hiked, and did walking meditations every day while also spending time with my family. After a few weeks, I was able to let go of my attachment to the idea of immediately getting a new job. With my expectations gone, my time off turned into a wonderful five-month sabbatical with my family, and during that time job offers kept coming in without me even looking.

We expect a lot from all those around us. I have expectations that my dogs will behave when I take them for a walk. I have expectations that my kids will be respectful and do well in school. I have expectations that I will get my paycheck on time each month. When our expectations are not met, our actions are a reaction to the negative emotions we feel due to not having our expectations met.

However big or small these situations may be, the cause of so much frustration, anger, and arguments in any relationship ultimately leads to this one question: Why haven't you met my expectations? No matter the relationship, whether it's a close friend, family member, spouse, or someone you barely know, it's important to always talk about expectations within the relationship. If it's a romantic relationship, talk about the next step after you move in. Can you each continue to go out with your friends, and if so, is there a curfew? Do you want to get married or have kids at some point? Who's doing the laundry? Are you sharing a bank account? What about doing the dishes? Both individuals in the relationship need to be clear with each other about how you see your life together once you start sharing the same bed; even that is an expectation in itself!

Every interaction we have with another human being comes with expectations, and our past experiences usually define what expectations we have. Sometimes we have expectations with uncertain origins, but they still dictate how we react to a situation. In these instances, you may be fighting a cause that you don't really care about, but because your expectations have not been met, you may continue fighting for this cause, which may eventually hurt your relationship.

Does it matter that the dishes were left in the sink last night? Does it matter that your friend couldn't make your birthday dinner even though she was surprised with an out-of-town trip planned with a new boyfriend? Think about what the expectation was and why you were upset. In the birthday dinner case, might you have been hurt because of your important expectation that she meet your family at this dinner? Or was it that she chose him over you? Or perhaps, having hinted to your boyfriend that you'd like a surprise trip, you had your own unmet expectation after no trip resulted. If the latter was the case, then once you realize this, you may no longer be mad at your friend.

The next time you are upset at someone or a particular situation, think about what your expectations were. Steer away from assuming those around you know what your expectations are. Talk about your expectations with the other person involved. Evaluate *why* you are having those expectations and what it is you really want before asking someone to meet them. And also consider what expectations the other person may have and try to understand that person's side as well.

I spent my entire life living by expectations that were consistently never met. As a consequence, I went through life repeating my mantra: *Why me? It's not fair.* As I changed my beliefs around those expectations, I learned that understanding your expectations, talking about them, and letting go of your attachment to them can bring something of much more value to you in the long run.

HATE AND OTHER NEGATIVE THINKING—I used to hate most things in my life, and I said it often. I hate my dad. I hate work. I hate this dinner. I hate my ex-husband. The word "hate" is used so often in our society for even the slightest of things. It's an intense word to describe something so meaningless most of the time, and what people don't realize is that most of the damage from using that word is not to the receiver, but to oneself.

The Merriam-Webster Dictionary defines the word "hate" as "intense hostility and aversion usually deriving from fear, anger, or sense of injury" or an "extreme dislike or disgust."

I no longer say the word "hate," and I try not to hate anything. KRS-One is a rapper from the eighties who has spent the last ten years or so speaking on topics of the history of rap, culture, and religion. In my opinion, he's an amazing speaker, and one of the things he speaks about is knowledge and your vocabulary. KRS-One states that your perception, or what you see, is based on your knowledge, and your knowledge is based on your vocabulary. I like to apply this concept to negative thinking. If your vocabulary includes negative words such as "hate," "disgust," "lies," "deception," "stupid," "annoyance," and so on, then that will continue to be your perception of those things you describe. If your vocabulary includes positive words such as "love," "hope," "beautiful," "compassion," and "patience," then what you perceive in your life will be exactly that.

When I used "hate" in the past, it brought up negative feelings inside me, so I chose not to use it any longer. The practice of positive speaking doesn't mean you are ignoring the negative side of a circumstance. Instead, you are acknowledging the situation and taking a different perspective so it doesn't impact you by causing a negative reaction:

"My dad was not a great dad, but he did the best he knew how as a father. He provided us with food and a roof over our heads and made me the strong, independent woman I am today."

"Work is good, and if I don't like what I'm doing, I have the choice to change my circumstances."

"I am grateful for this dinner, even if I don't like it, since I am fortunate to be able to eat."

With practice I now rarely use "hate" to describe anything, and when I do, I immediately correct myself and change my thinking.

The next time you say a negative word, see what emotions it brings up in you. Does it make you physically ill? Does it make you angry? How does that emotion drive your thinking or actions? If you're angry at the cashier for taking too long to check you out, you may be thinking to yourself, *I hate this cashier,* and storm off in anger. But if you can change your vocabulary to something positive, how might you react in return? When you have that thought, correct yourself and say, *I don't hate this cashier. I don't like that it's taking this long, but I don't need to be in such a hurry, so I will focus on patience.* Can you feel the difference in the emotion inside of you? How does your thinking or action change because of it? Instead of leaving the store in anger, you will probably leave in a much better frame of mind. It's easy to change your perspective on even the simplest of things just by changing your choice of words.

If you are struggling to turn those negative words into positive ones, try meditation. Spend a few minutes thinking about why you are feeling those negative feelings and try to see it from a different perspective. You can do this in a quiet room or even while driving your car. While driving, turn your radio off and focus your thoughts on your negative thinking completely (while still paying attention to your driving!).

Accept your thoughts of negativity and know that it is in your current nature to think those thoughts. Don't apply guilt or shame to them, just acknowledgment, and let them flow through your mind.

Then dissolve your thoughts by asking yourself, *Where are these thoughts coming from? How do they make me feel?* Break it down until you have found the core of your emotions and thoughts. *What is the real cause behind these negative thoughts?* Give it some time, and you will find that piece of the puzzle.

And then, finally, *solve it*! Now that you understand the true source of your negative thinking, what actions can you take to fix the situation in a more positive way? Perhaps the only action is to send love and compassion instead of negative thinking to the person.

The more you practice positive speaking, the more your reactions change in the form of positive actions and the more they become your nature.

PARENTHOOD—When my kids were little and we were having a rough day, I would say to them, "No one ever gave me a book on how to be a parent. I'm doing the best I can!" Obviously, there are a lot of books on how to parent, but who's to say that any of them are right? Parenting comes with its challenges, and no one book is a perfect fit for any parent. As I always say in the corporate world, "There is best practice, and then there is best fit for an organization." Before I became a parent, I was very judgmental of other parents and had my own thoughts about how to be the perfect parent. It took me having my own kids to realize that each family has its own challenges and parents must do whatever is the best fit for their family.

I have talked about both the good and the bad parenting choices I have made as a mother. I've found over the years that I have not been alone in those choices. The stress of parenting can force us to behave in ways that we may not be proud of, even when we think we are doing what's best for our kids.

Through my transformation, I learned to be more loving and patient with myself and think more positively toward others. With this change I realized that I also have a lot more love and patience for my kids. No one book will give you the answers on how to raise the "perfect child" or be the "perfect parent," but taking care of yourself first will help you love and care for your children the best you can.

In recent years I've had conversations with several sets of friends who were having their first child. They all told me how scared they were of raising a child and how much stress they put on themselves to be a good parent before the baby was even born! I found myself offering words of parenting advice, and what I found was that six months or even a year later these same friends told me they remembered my advice and learned to effectively use it to remind themselves to ease the pressure they put on themselves.

1) Everyone is going to offer you advice—take what works for you and throw out the rest. Every child is different, so you must adjust your rules and plans accordingly. When my kids were little, I'd take advice from experienced friends or from a book I read and try to use it, but it didn't always work. When my son would start crying at night as an infant, the advice I read was to "let him cry it out." After days of sitting outside his door as he screamed and I cried, I knew that advice was not going to work for me. Another one was this: "Don't ever let your kids sleep in your bed." When I was going through my divorce, having my kids sleep in my bed was both comforting for me as well as them. No one knows your family better than you do, so hear it all, but take only what's useful.

2) Sleep when your baby sleeps. This is important, not just when your child is a baby, but also when the kids are grown. The message here is that you must be well rested so that you can have more quality time with your children. For example, if you are busy doing laundry and cleaning up messes while your infant child sleeps, then you will be even more exhausted and have less patience with the child when he or she is awake. When the children are older, the same can be applied to when and how you run your errands, work, clean house, and do whatever it is that keeps you busy. Try to do those tasks when your kids are busy with other activities, be it in school, at a friend's house, or asleep. When my kids were younger, I told them too many times, "I'm too busy." And it took separation from them during my divorce to realize that the time I spent with them needed to be quality time bonding and making a connection. As my kids grow older, I take the same advice, and when I am with them, I am spending quality time with them rather than doing other busywork that keeps me from having conversations with them.

3) **Put your adult relationship first**—*it's what gives your children a solid foundation.* Whatever your circumstances may be, the adults in the house who are raising the kids must have a strong relationship. Your situation could be a couple, grandmother/daughter, mother/caretaker, father/friend. Regardless of what that adult relationship is, it's the foundation your kids are learning from. That foundation must send a message of love, trust, support, and reassurance for your kids. My first husband and I did not put our relationship first, and that led to our family coming apart in the end.

And most importantly, whether or not you are in a relationship, putting yourself first is key to having a strong foundation for your kids to depend on. One night when I was making dinner, I made my plate first and my husband, Mike, called me out on it. My response was jokingly, "A mother lion always feeds herself first before her cubs so she can stay strong for her kids." While my family didn't think it was as funny as I did, I meant it. You have to take care of yourself first, then your adult relationship, then your kids—having a strong foundation for them is critical to being more present for them.

4) Don't have guilt or regret for what you do as a parent. Unless you are hurting your child, having guilt or regret for how you live your life and raise your child does your child no good. When my kids didn't like my rules and we would fight, I would tell them, "You can talk about it in therapy when you are older!" (which they are now actually doing thanks to behaviors they learned from me in my earlier years). However, I don't have guilt or regret about those days.

When they were young, I traveled a lot for work, and when I was home, I wasn't there for them because I was too caught up in my own self-pity. I didn't think I gave them what they needed, but maybe I did. I am who I am today because of the strengths my father gave me, regardless of how he raised me.

My father still has a lot of guilt and regret for how he raised us, and yet I like who I am. I wouldn't be the strong, independent, and confident woman I am today had he raised me differently. And as my relationship with my father was "predetermined," my kids and I also agreed to come to this earth together and take this course—it's what we signed up for. While I could have been more present with my kids in the early years, what happened was exactly how it was intended to play out, and all I can do is learn from it and move forward in a positive way in my relationship with them.

5) Trust your instincts. When my son was four months old, he cried out in what I thought was pain when he peed. I went to his pediatrician several times and was told I was overreacting and my baby was fine. I finally made them do a urinalysis, and it turned out he had an infection. At four months old, my son had surgery to correct a blocked kidney valve. Don't let anyone else or any book or doctor tell you that you are wrong. As a parent, you know your child better than anyone else, so trust yourself, and act on what your instincts tell you.

6) Don't try to keep up with other parents. Many kids today are playing two or three sports a season, taking music lessons, and doing all kinds of other activities to live up to their parents' plans of what they want them to be. I always struggle with wanting to give my kids the best opportunities for success but at the same time being fearful that if I push them in one direction I may limit them from other amazing things they could possibly achieve.

My kids are not overbooked with after-school activities. When other parents talk about all the activities and achievements of their kids, I always joke, "I accept the fact that my kids are mediocre." My kids are far from mediocre—they are smart and intelligent, and I learn from them every day. When my boys were younger, a psychic told me that I had two children, an indigo child and a rainbow child. Indigo and rainbow children are part of a larger category of children called star children. There is one more child type called the crystal child. These star children have different characteristics of coming to this planet and have unique abilities such as being extremely empathetic, more aware of their surroundings, and wiser than most kids or even adults, and sometimes they come here with remembered experiences of past lives.

I had no idea what those terms were when the psychic told me at the time, but I tried to keep an open mind. When we got home that night my older son, Tino, was playing video games. I had never given much attention to the screen name he'd picked out when he was five years old. I never gave it much thought, although I did think it was a bit feminine at the time. I had forgotten about it altogether until that night, and when I saw his screen name I was floored: "Rainbow crystal." Tino always talked about "not fitting in." He had a lot of friends, but he would state he felt as if he was from somewhere else, not of this earth. He had empathy for the weaker and younger kids and for animals. Was that just a coincidence?

My younger son, Joey, used to write and tell many stories and adventures of what seemed like a past life living in wartime. He also drew very technical and detailed drawings of electronics all over his body and could tell you how it all functioned. Whenever things were going badly, Joey would say to me, "I'll sit next to you because I'm your positive energy"—even though I had never spoken those types of words in the house before. Or he would say, "God is on my side—I know that"—when we never spoke those words in the house.

My kids may not be in sports or have their days full of school activities and clubs, but even as young adults their intelligence astounds me, and I look forward to what adventures their lives will lead them to.

7) Practice detachment with your kids. When my kids were little, the stresses of life and raising a family would frustrate me, and I'd take my anger out on them. One day I thought about my nieces as well as my friends' kids and wondered why I didn't get frustrated with them. Whenever I interacted with them, I saw them as individuals. I was engaged, listening, and talking with them and saw them with different eyes. I realized it was because I was detached from them. I had no expectations from these kids, so they didn't frustrate me. I decided to practice that with my son one day. While we were lying on the floor reading a book, I detached myself from him. I looked at him as an individual and thought, *What if he wasn't my child?* In that moment I saw my child in a very different light. I was able to see him for who he really was. Whenever my "mom moments" come back, I try to take a step back and see them for who they really are, and those are the times I find they are teaching me and we are having the best moments together.

Parenting has its challenges, and there will always be pressures from others on how you should raise your kids. In an earlier chapter of my life, I wrote this in my journal about my kids when I was having a bad day: "How will they sum me up in one sentence when they are older?" My advice to myself and other parents is this: just love them, do your best, and hope that if they can sum you up in one sentence at the end of your life that it's a positive one.

LIVING OUTSIDE YOUR BOX—Being raised first-generation American in a Sicilian household, I was told that women didn't work—they married and had kids. You cooked, cleaned, did laundry, and took care of your man and children. That was the "box" assigned to me when I was a child, and I fought it every step of the way. I saw my mom unhappy in her role, and I wanted more for myself—to be independent and provide for myself, to not be dependent on a man to provide me with my needs.

In the beginning I was angry at my parents for placing this box around me for how I should live my life. When my father didn't pay for my college at the school where I wanted to go, I became the victim of my circumstances and blamed him for my not being able to achieve my dreams. Even when he turned around and offered to pay for community college, I kept the victim theme going by dropping out after only two semesters. My thought process and the blame I put on my father allowed me to stay in the box that they'd put me in. Luckily, my passion took another path and I was able to succeed on my own without my parents' help once I decided I was independent enough to take control.

Living outside your box doesn't mean you have to make big changes all at once. Each day you can commit yourself to taking one step closer to reaching your goals. Here are some of the small steps I've taken on my path to make those big changes over time.

When I was a kid, one of my favorite things to do was read *Reader's Digest* and *TV Guide*. I would read them from beginning to end until I had each page memorized and I could tell you about all the stories I had read and what our favorite TV shows were going to be about. Actually, I read them from end to front, starting from the last page and reading the pages in reverse until I got to page one, which is something I still do today when I read magazines. This behavior was due to my dyslexia, something I didn't learn about myself until my adulthood. My sister would joke that I was a computer, and while I was reading, she would walk around our living room saying, "Computer, buzz, buzz." She must have known something because this was in the seventies, before "computers" were a household name.

As a young girl I would take apart radios and anything I could get my hands on and look at every part like it was the most incredible object ever. Trying to figure out how something worked was so interesting to me. My interest in technology over the years grew as I learned about electric typewriters, then computers. I taught myself programming when there were very few females in the industry. This was all new technology at the time, but I was enjoying learning something new. I applied myself to becoming the best I could be at it. With each new skill learned, I sought out jobs that stretched my skills, and I took risks to see if I could succeed. Slowly, over time, I was building a foundation for my strengths and skills that brought me to my career today, only I didn't realize it at the time. I was following my passion and looking for opportunities all around me. During this time I was working a full-time job, working in retail part-time, and continuing to work on my home business. I was determined to be successful and not be dependent on any man for my wants.

Some of the most successful leaders spend five hours a week reading and learning about something new, including Bill Gates, Elon Musk, and former president Barack Obama. Thomas C. Corley is the author of *Rich Habits: The Daily Success Habits of Wealthy Individuals,* and he states that one of the common aspects of successful individuals is that they spend at least thirty minutes or more a day reading or learning for self-education.

That book was not around when I was a kid, but I have always held those habits of constantly learning about something new.

Over the years I have worked in software development, technical training, consulting, and IT management. I recently heard that men in business look for advancement and new career opportunities based on what they want to do, not based on what skills they currently have, while women, on the other hand, wait until they have the skills and experience to take on new opportunities. I've taken risks in the past, and this has provided me consistent growth opportunities. Women tend to think, *I'm not good enough. I don't have the experience. I have no idea how to do that role.* But taking risks, with the added work of learning about where you are headed along the way, is the path to moving forward. Remind yourself: *You are good enough! You have the skills to be successful! You have the strength to take that next step!* It's that positive talk to yourself that will guide you in your next steps, whether the steps you take are related to work, personal relationships, or anything else you have your mind set on.

I've enjoyed my career and really have a passion for what I do. I never finished college, but I've far surpassed my goals of being a secretary to the rock stars. That was because I took a huge leap out of the box that my parents had assigned to me.

In the beginning, I was following my passion to remove myself from my past, to succeed and become something greater than the life that had been laid out for me. It wasn't about money, and I didn't have a plan for how I was going to be successful. I just knew I had to work hard and focus on being successful day-to-day. My only goal was to never be dependent on anyone, especially a man, to take care of me. My parents were hard workers, and all of my siblings and I took on a similar work ethic. We always had at least two jobs, and we took pride in our work. My work defined me since it was the only definition I knew how to give myself at the time.

Everyone's box is different and is defined by those who raised that person and those around that person. Whether it's work or personal success, it's up to you to define what success looks like. Stepping out of your box will almost always bring along challenges and judgments. My career does not define me, but I'm proud of what I have achieved. I am a woman working in a predominantly male field of technology, not always an equal playing field on the road to success. I am grateful for the teaching and mentoring opportunities given to me and for those that I can provide to others. I'm still always learning as I continue to grow in my field.

As a young girl, I had lost all hope of the smallest dreams when my parents handed my future to me in a predefined box. I climbed out of that box, challenging as that climb was, and anyone else can do it too. I've been married, divorced, and remarried, along with having kids and building a career. This path came with its obstacles and many opinions along the way, but I pushed forward, driven by my own instincts.

It's easy to take for granted what is right in front of you and the hard road it took to get there. Whatever you may be doing that pays the bills or otherwise fills your days, remember where you've been and how far you've come. And remember that no matter how unsatisfied you are with it, your current situation may be what takes you unknowingly to your next adventure. If you're unhappy with where you are, set your goals and then leap out of your box.

PROTECTING THE BULLY—As I explained in an earlier chapter, I was a bully. I was a childhood bully, a bully to my own kids when I was going through tough times, and a bully to my ex-husband. I learned to overcome that, but there are many adults who are still bullies. People, especially kids, can be mean-spirited. They learn that behavior from other kids, and most importantly, they also learn it from their parents. If a child is a bully, we need to not punish the child but learn what in the environment is causing that child to be a bully. As a child, I was abused and angry, and I took my anger out on other kids. It was a call for help that continued to go unanswered.

Kids these days are committing suicide at an alarming rate because of bullying, and the age of suicides is getting younger and younger. The internet doesn't help either. When a kid is bullied now, it's not just in front of a few classmates—it becomes visible to the entire world. Hundreds of millions of kids and parents join in on the harassment.

As a society, this needs to stop. We need to set an example for all kids and all other human beings. A child bully is angry, sad, depressed, or abused. It is a learned behavior, a self-defense for the abuse that child is getting either at home or somewhere in the environment. Such a child is taught this behavior by an adult bully or perhaps the unfortunate circumstances of a particular living environment. With no parent to blame, the child may be angry or ashamed because of certain living situations: no home, living with a family out of a car, or starving from lack of food.

I didn't realize I was a bully until I became an adult. Some of you may be bullying your own kids and not even realize it, or your kids may be bullied at school by their classmates. If this is happening, recognize it for what it is.

We need to start protecting the bullies, even if that bully is you it's you that needs to start protecting yourself. Seek help. There are a lot of organizations available to help you if you find the stresses of daily life are affecting you and how you react to others. There are many places to go for safety if you feel you, your kids, or even someone else's kids are in an unhealthy living environment. We need to examine each incident carefully to understand what is causing this behavior, and we need to seek help from organizations that support these kids—organizations that didn't exist when I was a child.

Learn from my experiences, and let's help one another other at these times. Let's be gentle to these kids and find out what is driving them to bully others. And let's teach all kids and adults to show how kindness, love, and compassion are more effective ways to interact with each other.

OWN YOUR HEALTH—When Tino was five years old, he started having meltdowns in which he would cry and couldn't stop. A trigger would be that he had gotten in trouble or was upset with a toy or frustrated by his brother—typical childhood frustrations. But once he started crying, he couldn't stop himself. I'd try to console him to stop his crying, and he would respond, "I can't stop crying. I don't know why, but I can't stop crying." The sheer mention of that would make him cry more.

I started to notice a trend that his crying meltdowns were usually after he had drunk too much milk. Tino seemed thirsty all the time, and he loved milk. He would drink two, three, or more glasses in one evening. My intuition was telling me that the milk was causing his meltdowns. I'm not saying that milk's effects are bad for everyone. For me, milk has had a positive effect—I drank it regularly two days before and after my menstrual cycle to successfully ward off headaches. My mother and Tino's dad didn't believe me when I suggested the milk might be causing the issues. "That's crazy," they said. "Milk is good for you. How can milk make him cry?" We fought about it a lot, and I would try and keep my son from drinking too much milk. I noticed a difference when I was able to limit the amount he was drinking, but I was consistently overruled when his grandma or father gave in to his pleas for more.

Several years later, my husband, Mike, picked up a book by Datis Kharrazian called *Why Isn't My Brain Working?* The book's focus is about how the food you eat affects not only your physical self but your mental state as well. I was intrigued. I'd had food issues most of my life and had always blamed them on my father for "breaking me." My health issues had gotten worse as I was entering menopause. In less than a year, I had put on over thirty-five pounds, my hair was falling out in clumps, and I couldn't sleep at night since I was getting up every two hours to pee or I was waking up drenched in sweat from hot flashes.

During this time my food allergies were exacerbated, and everything I ate made me itch, caused me to feel lightheaded and dizzy, and gave me severe headaches. My stomach pains were strong, and pills no longer helped. I had been working long hours at work, and taking care of myself was not a priority. After two years of ignoring my health needs, my poor physical health was starting to affect my mental health. I cried at how helpless I felt with all my ills. I finally went to a doctor when my thyroid was out of control. My medication dosage was changed five times over the next year as I sought out five different doctors regarding my menopause. Each doctor laughed it off. "Deal with it," they told me. "Take hormone pills," they also said. But I was done with pills. I wanted to fix myself the natural way.

I decided to read for myself the book Mike had brought home. It's not an easy read. It uses a lot of medical jargon. I didn't understand it all, but it changed my thoughts about food and mental health. I remembered my son and his issues with milk. If certain foods affected my son's mental health, as I had believed, then maybe my poor mental health, the years of depression and sadness, could also have been partly caused by the foods I was eating. "Functional medicine," as Datis Kharrazian calls it, is the connection of the foods we eat and our mental health. It's about finding the cause of your physical health issues rather than just fixing the symptoms. I knew I had been just fixing my symptoms all those years, so I continued to research the topic of functional medicine. The more I read about it, the more I knew that this was one of the things I needed to do to get myself healthy.

One of the first things I did was ditch the alcohol altogether. On and off, alcohol had consumed most of my life, and when I had been drinking, both my mental and physical state had deteriorated. While I had stopped drinking heavily at this point, even one glass of wine would have its effect on me, so I no longer wanted it to be part of my life. I wrote down all the reasons why I didn't want to drink and put the list next to my bed: "Drunk, depressed, sensitive, jealous, sick, nauseous, agitated, anxious, can't sleep." I still keep the list in my nightstand drawer as a reminder. I chose to stop drinking more than two years ago, and I don't miss it or think about it ever since I enjoy having a clear head to focus on more important things in my life.

After much searching for the right doctor and program, with some failures in this area, I found a doctor who practiced functional medicine whom I felt I could trust. Dr. Christopher Mote has a practice in functional medicine in Colorado and has surrounded himself with a great team dedicated to helping men and women like me on a nontraditional path of becoming healthy using functional medicine. The program involves a holistic view of your lifestyle and includes education on health in the form of individual and group classes, with topics such as eating healthy foods, balancing work and exercise, using stress management, and even monitoring and adjusting sleeping patterns. I also met with a nutritionist to work on my food issues. We were able to determine that I had excessive inflammation in my body, and its cause was the foods that I was eating. I had to change my diet completely. I was determined to stick to the plan so that I could feel better.

Mike also gave me another book. This one was from Louise Hay and called *You Can Heal Your Life*. It's about how negative thought patterns create sickness in your physical self. The book tells the story of Louise Hay and how she cured herself of cancer using positive thinking and affirmations. It outlines illnesses and probable causes with affirmations or new thought patterns to help you change your thinking and cure those illnesses.

I looked up inflammation and stomach problems and found the following:

INFLAMMATION
Probable cause: *Fear, seeing red. Inflamed thinking.*
New thought pattern: *My thinking is peaceful, calm, and centered.*

STOMACH PAINS
Probable cause: *Dread. Fear of the new. Inability to assimilate the new.*
New thought pattern: *Life agrees with me. I assimilate the new every moment of every day. All is well.*

I wasn't sure why I was feeling those feelings because, other than being sick, I managed a balanced work-life schedule, and life at home was good. I had started my yoga and meditation practices again, so in my meditations I focused on these feelings. It was then that I recognized that I had recently completed a project at work and had been expecting a promotion that never came. I was frustrated with my work since my expectation had not been met. I had been thinking about quitting my job, yet I had fear about starting again in a new job. I practiced those affirmations, along with several others, each morning, repeating them as I looked at myself in the mirror.

In less than a year, with my affirmations and my changed diet, I lost thirty-five pounds. I no longer have food issues. My hair stopped falling out and has grown back healthier than it ever has been, and I sleep peacefully every night. My thyroid medication has actually been lowered, and I take a few daily supplements on a regular basis. For the first time in fifty years, I can eat without anticipation of feeling sick. I have eliminated all grains, soy, bovine dairy foods, legumes, and processed foods from my diet, but I still eat what I want within those boundaries.

Since I missed eating the foods I'd grown up with, I decided to convert my mom's homemade pasta and pizza recipes to meet my food-restriction criteria while tasting just as delicious as the originals. I eat ice cream on a regular basis, something I had not been able to do in years—now I eat it made from cashew, almond, or coconut milk instead of cow's milk. I have more energy and feel better than I have in my entire life. My motto of "Always eat, and you will feel great" is finally a reality. I eat a lot, all day long, since I still love my food. As long as it is within my list of acceptable foods, I feel great. My mind is no longer racing with fears about what I put into my mouth and the reaction my body will have toward it. How freeing! (Do note that these diet changes are specifically meant for me alone to address my health issues under a supervised physician and nutritionist. Please do not take this as advice on how you should eat for yourself.)

Louise's book helps me a lot these days. Whenever I am sick or my back hurts or I have a toothache, a cold, or a cold sore, I look in the book. It gives me a probable cause and then a new thought pattern—an affirmation to say every day, several times a day, until I change my thinking and get well. It may sound crazy, but I can almost always relate to the probable cause, and when

I do the affirmations, they honestly work. I find that after a few days, I am better.

Now that I am of healthy mind and my body is no longer a burden, I look back and know that I was sick for so many years because I allowed myself to be. There are studies that link the effects of certain foods with Alzheimer's disease, dementia, autism, depression, diabetes, and other various diseases. One could argue that the mental and physical debilities I experienced were related to the foods I ate as part of my upbringing. Were my depression, sadness, and stomach pains side effects of the foods I consumed? Or did my victim mindset create a sickness in both my body and mind?

It's the chicken or the egg argument. What's important is that taking care of your body is just as important as taking care of your mind. And I've learned how to take care of both.

As we age, our ailments get worse as our bodies start to deteriorate. Most of us tend to look to others to fix us, and I was no exception. We eat burritos and take a pill to keep from having reflux. We eat sugar and take pills for diabetes. We indulge in alcohol and fried foods and then take blood pressure medicine or pills for high cholesterol. We do not educate ourselves on how to prevent our bodies from failing, and our go-to response is to treat the symptoms with pills and unnecessary surgeries instead of fixing the causes themselves. Some modern medicine is still bewitchery, and in the future, it may be looked upon no differently than a bottle of snake oil. Being mentally and physically healthy is at least partly a matter of a person's mind-set.

But then again, it's all choice. We have the choice to indulge, and that's also the joy of living, isn't it? I recently took a trip back home to New York for a wedding. I knew before I left that

I would eat pizza, chicken egg foo young, a bagel with lox and cream cheese, and a bacon, egg, and cheese sandwich on a kaiser roll. Only New York offers the best of these foods. I had the opportunity to eat all of it except the egg foo young. I got sick with stomach pains after each meal, but boy did I enjoy the hell out of eating them while in the moment! It was the most delicious food I had eaten in a long time!

PERFECTIONIST NO MORE—No one is exactly perfect, me included, and I am constantly looking at ways to help myself. I read self-help books regularly, and I listen to motivational podcasts on my way to work. I am always researching topics on physical and mental health. Knowledge is power, and learning and taking action regarding my own health, and seeing the results, is what keeps me motivated

In recent months my husband and I have been arguing quite a bit about my obsessive-compulsive disorder (OCD). Apparently, I'm demonstrating a lot of OCD-type behaviors lately, and the constant fidgeting is driving him nuts. I don't even realize it. I don't think it's anything new—I think he's just noticing it more. He, of course, disagrees. So now I'm focusing on working through my OCD.

I recently read information from the Anxiety and Depression Association of America (ADAA) that said OCD is rooted in anxiety and distress. The OCD actions are to ease the thoughts around that anxiety and distress. I started asking myself these questions: If anxiety is typically based on fear, what fear did I have that caused me to check the lock three times before I went to bed each night? Was it that I didn't trust myself that I was safe? Would checking the lock three times make me feel any safer? After thinking about it, I realized I was still operating in fear on some level.

FEAR can be an acronym for "fake experience appearing real," or "false evidence appearing real." In reading this, I found my cure. Each time I think to check a lock, I think to myself, *Fake experience appearing real*—and I immediately no longer need to check it. These days the thoughts come less and less frequently into my head because I have been able to break the habit I created out of fear. I've stopped the counting, and I've stopped the door checking. That's a big improvement for me. Next, I need to figure out the fidgeting, and I realize as I write this that I could meditate on it!

I like to think of myself as perfectly imperfect. What's considered perfect for one individual is imperfection for another and vice versa. We all have choices on how we live our life on this earth, and as long as we aren't hurting others and treat each other with love and respect, then each of us should decide what his or her perfect self is.

I still

- *smoke a few cigarettes a day*
- *have OCD*
- *have dyslexia*
- *occasionally eat foods that make me sick*
- *have sensitive skin*
- *and have aches and pains.*

Yet I no longer let these imperfections consume me. They're no longer a mindfuck.

If I find something about my body that is taking up too much energy and I'm talking to myself about it, I work to let it go. I listen to my physical self and take care of it as best I can. I accept my body. What I used to see as a burden, I am now grateful for since my body allows me to enjoy life here on this earth.

WE ARE ALL BEAUTIFUL—When I was a young girl, I never felt beautiful. Skinny and cute I was—and short. I always had a little belly, and even in my teens, strangers would ask me, "Are you pregnant?" Unlike the girlfriend of Bruce Willis's character in *Pulp Fiction,* who wanted a little pot belly like Madonna, I did not like my pot belly. I tried to like what I saw in the mirror, but as my body was my burden, I saw it in its entirety and didn't like how I felt and what I saw. I saw a broken-down body, ugly and unloved. I remember buying *Cosmopolitan* magazines. The models were so beautiful, and I was envious not only of their beauty but of their health. In my mind I would picture them on the toilet taking a poo. That always made me laugh because it reminded me that they were just as human as I was.

Recently, I decided to stop coloring my hair and let my freak flag fly. I have had gray hair since I was a kid; it started as a long two-inch-wide gray stripe on the side of my head that I was born with. My nickname was "Silver Streak." By the time I was thirty-five, I had a lot of gray, and I began coloring it regularly. What started as every three months eventually turned into every two weeks. I would spend my Saturday mornings coloring the landing strip that always appeared so quickly. Another mindfuck.

Coloring my hair seemed as uncomfortable as having a hot flash in a crowded room; it looked obvious and intentional, and I felt like a fake. The pressure to stay "looking young" as a woman can be difficult to overcome. I remember telling my mom that when I was fifty, I was going to stop coloring my hair, and she gasped. "Don't stop coloring your hair," she said. "You still look so young!" When fifty came, I couldn't do it and gave into peer pressure instead. Still working in a corporate environment, I was concerned about looking old, so I changed my goal to sixty.

During menopause something changed in me, and I just couldn't do it any longer. So just before my fifty-third birthday, I excitedly made the decision to go for it. I haven't wavered since. With the help of my hairstylist, Angela, whom I pressured into helping me go through this transformation, I now have my natural gray-and-white hair. I love it, and I feel as powerful as Gandalf the White, the wizard from *The Lord of the Rings: The Two Towers*. Like the caterpillar in Pixar's *A Bug's Life* proudly proclaims, "I am a beautiful butterfly!" That has become another new mantra for me. My hair is as authentic as I am; it's the real me, my true self.

Who cares what people think anyhow? The response has been positive both at home and at work. Most importantly, I love whom I see when I look in the mirror.

These days, I love what I see in myself, and I notice beauty in everyone, no matter what they look like. I feel great, and more importantly, I feel healthy. My body is no longer a burden. Taking guidance from Louise Hay, I look in the mirror and daily say, "I love you; you are beautiful." We are all beautiful, inside and out, and don't let anyone or society in general tell you otherwise.

DEFINE YOUR HAPPINESS—For me, happiness is a peaceful mind and spending time with my family. For others, and I was once one of them, it's money, career, and material things. I recently read that many people, when they pray for themselves, usually say stuff like, "Please, God, let me get that promotion. Please, God, I need more money. Please, God, I want a new car." But when we pray for other people, it's usually that they be happy, healthy, and safe.

It wasn't until I started focusing on those same prayers for myself and for others that I found happiness. The material things are unimportant. I'm grateful to have a house and food anytime I am hungry. I'm grateful to have a warm shower and a toilet. I'm grateful for a career I enjoy and the car that I drive. But those things are unimportant. Like my husband always says, "I've never seen a U-Haul being pulled by a hearse."

When my kids were younger, we would watch TV together, and some shows on *Animal Planet* or *National Geographic* would highlight a culture very different from ours. There would be families in third-world countries living in huts or shacks with no running water or electricity and no easy access to food. I would provoke conversation with my kids and ask them questions such as "What do those kids have in common with you?" or "What do those families have in common with us?" We'd talk about their smiles and how they laughed and played jokes like we did. We would note that the kids were playing games with each other in the street even though none wore shoes and the streets were dirt. They did not have the same stresses over matters such as work, who was driving the kids to soccer, or "who took my favorite-color crayon." They did not have what we considered basic necessities, yet they were happy.

What is the meaning of happiness? For each of us it's different, and many of us don't even know what happiness is for ourselves because we are too distracted moving through our lives like robots adhering to a script given to us as children, the script that will give us that happily-ever-after ending. Look deep into yourself and define what your happiness looks like to you. Knowing what that is will help you determine what your path might be to get there.

My happiness is peace. Peace of mind, peace of body. Positivity and surrounding myself with those things that maintain my peace. When you are depressed, you surround yourself with things and are detached from people; when you are healthy, you are detached from stuff and want to show love to people around you.

The older I get, the more I purge. Stuff takes up useless energy cleaning, organizing, buying, selling, and thinking about, so I purge what I'm tired of cleaning. I purge negativity—whether it's people, TV shows, the news, environments, objects that invoke negative thoughts, or even something as simple as a broken kitchen tool.

A few months ago, I bought a cookie scoop that broke after just a few times of use. Since I'd just bought it, I refused to throw it out and tried to force it to work. But every time I used it, as I scooped the cookie dough, the gears would be misaligned, and the dough would not drop out. I tried fixing it more than once until I finally threw it out. So small a thing, yet so frustrating. How it consumed my thoughts and energy. Why was I wasting so much time talking to myself about how wasteful it would be to throw it out? Then I realized I didn't have to waste that time any longer.

Whatever this thing might be, if it annoys you every time you encounter it, it's creating a negative emotion that is useless and creates a negative effect on your mind and body. The same goes with people. If anyone stirs negativity in me so that I feel deflated, exhausted, or physically ill, I choose to no longer be around that person. Detach yourself from those things. Life is short, so I surround myself with positive people and experiences.

The same goes for the reverse since I hold myself to the same standards. How do I want to affect people today? I was once in a yoga class and our instructor asked, "What color is your paintbrush?" He described how each day when we walk out to the world, we should think of ourselves as a paintbrush, dripping wet with paint. Everywhere we go, we leave that color because we're painting all around us. That morning he told us that he had snapped at someone at the grocery store on his way to teach his class and that person had snapped back at him. He realized then that his paintbrush was gray, and he knew he had to change colors before class.

My paintbrush is not always bright yellow, my favorite color, but I try to keep it that way (and when I don't, I have my husband and kids to remind me!). We all interact with each other, and one touch of gray paint by one person can affect dozens of people in a day. We pass on what we carry, whether that's anger, sadness, or happiness. Imagine what a world we would live in if we could all paint yellow every day!

5

EVERYDAY BEING

WHEN YOU CHANGE your perspective on life, it's amazing how it can change not only how you view your future but also how you view your past. My past is no longer divided by chapters, and the shame of those pages has long gone way. In the song "Come with Me," the artist Nneka asks her country to surrender its pride and be truthful about the wrongs they have committed against their own people. Yet even with surrender, those experiences do not go away. They make up your soul and are part of who you are. It's as important to know where you have come from as it is where you are headed.

When I was younger, I saw negativity all around me. I didn't think God existed because of my past—how could he? Yet now I see good that comes from all things negative, and I have a different perspective on things. For many of us, our default behavior leans toward negativity—anger, jealousy, sadness, judgment. And I am still no different. But it's how we got to those feelings and the actions we take as a result that are important.

I based my life's actions and made decisions based on my perceived reality that I was a victim. Life can be difficult at times, and I have much more to learn. I still struggle through communication and, most importantly, finding compassion and empathy at times. My ways of working through the negativity are through meditation, contemplation, and mindfulness. I don't watch TV shows that are negative or violent. I never say the word "hate." I am always learning, always reading. The books I read have common themes of self-awareness and finding peace and compassion. I try to see people through to their souls rather than what's on the surface. I love reading the memoirs of others since we all have our own adversities that challenge us, and we have much to offer others as we learn to overcome these challenges. I do these things to stay happy, and when I am not aligned, my mind closes off, and the default behavior returns.

I am easily affected by sadness at times. Recently, Kate Spade committed suicide. On the day she died, I was wearing shoes she had designed, as probably many women were. They were a pair of black, high-heeled sandals I hadn't worn since the summer before. It was a beautiful, warm day as I put on those heels and a summer dress. As I headed out to work, I felt great and happy. A typical day at the office was awaiting me. When a colleague told me about her death, I couldn't stop thinking about it, but since I was busy all day with work, it was filed away in the back of my consciousness.

That night, going to sleep, I couldn't stop thinking about her and became overwhelmed with sadness. I was tired and no longer wanted to be on this earth. I prayed to my spirit guides to take me away in my sleep since I had nothing left to offer on this physical earth. This was not how I used to think about it when I was suicidal—this time it was different—still driven by sadness but more peaceful. I thought to myself, *Have I completed my course on earth? Is it time for me to move on?*

I surprised myself with these prayers, and yet I also asked not to be taken away. I was enjoying my life, but my default behavior was returning. I was confused in my thoughts that night until I finally fell asleep. The next day when I awoke, I was glad that I did. I'm not sure why her death had such an impact on me, but it was like I understood her; I empathized with her.

Several days later, celebrity chef Anthony Bourdain also committed suicide. I was a huge fan and was saddened by his death, but it did not impact me the way Kate's did. That night and every night for the next several nights, I prayed that I wouldn't feel this sadness. I prayed that I could stay on this earth and continue to be there for my husband, my kids, and me. I had so much to look forward to! And yet I didn't trust myself.

After a few days of prayer, I woke up one night with a sleep paralysis episode. I've had these most of my life, and they can be terrifying. This time it was especially surreal. I woke up in the middle of the night, lying on my stomach and feeling someone or something pulling at my legs. The entity was pulling so hard that it was lifting my legs in the air until I felt like they were so high I was doing a backbend while lying in bed. Then someone pulled at my arms.

It felt as if someone was sitting on my back and pulling both my legs and arms as high as they could. I tried to scream. During sleep paralysis, you are awake, yet you're still dreaming—perhaps it was a dream, or perhaps it was real. But it seemed very real since this entity was tugging at me. As I screamed, which would sound like a whimper to anyone around me, I felt my husband try to wake me out of this trance. As he did, the entity pulled so hard it seemed as if an entire energy lifted from inside of me and was pulled out. Then the entity was gone.

I was scared after this and called out to my spirit guides. They came immediately. My healer, usually in a black robe with a white light emanating from his face, appeared in the opposite garb—wearing a white robe with a black light where his face should have been. He then told me that they were pulling the sadness out of me as I had been asking them to, and all would be all right. I fell back asleep, and when I awoke the next day, the sadness had gone away.

What is it that brings me back to this place of sadness? I had been having a great day, and yet I had been so impacted by someone I knew nothing about. While I had a pair of the designer's shoes, it was the only pair. I knew nothing about her. I didn't even know what she looked like. For whatever reason, this is my default behavior. I have learned to use the tools and practices that I know to help me get through these times—meditation, prayer, energy work, and music. This default behavior, when it returns, is like treading water. I need to surround myself with positivity, or I start to drown. That week I played "Beauty in the World" by Macy Gray over and over in my car to use positive words to overcome those dark days. "Remember, God is giving you beauty in the world," she sings.

It's been ten years since I started my transformation process, and these days life is good. Each night as I go to sleep, I say a prayer and am grateful for the day. I have a loving family, a warm home, and a career I enjoy. My mind is at peace as I pray that I, my husband, our kids, and extended family are all safe and healthy and that we all find our happiness.

I feel healthier than I have in my entire life, both physically and mentally. I am very aware of listening to my body and mind to let me know when I am off-balance. I can easily be distracted by outside influences such as work and food, but I have a good support system around me, especially in my husband, to remind me to slow down when I am not fully taking care of myself.

I have found my faith and have become a very spiritual person. I have very strong beliefs regarding who I am and where I came from. I believe God exists and that we are all God. This life is an illusion, a true matrix, since our souls are illuminating energies that are part of a larger universe full of information and wisdom beyond what we know is real on this earth.

I once read an article about trees and the process of how their leaves drop. What I learned is that leaves don't fall off trees. Trees go through a process that actually pushes the leaves and then cuts the leaves off of them. If you watch closely, you can see individual leaves shaking and moving without wind. It's incredibly amazing to watch from this new viewpoint, as if the trees have consciousness like the trees in the movie *Avatar*. I notice this all the time now and wonder how much of the world around us is not as it seems. I see life as a classroom, as if each one of us is taking a course, each course a life on earth. Many of us know each other from before we arrived, and we came together with previous agreements we made to play out our roles and help each other in our lessons.

I continue to work on my goals and dreams while balancing my responsibilities. I am striving to be the best person I can be to myself and to my family in this lifetime. I've been sharing my new food recipes based on my diet changes with family and friends, and they have been encouraging me to write a blog or hold workshops on my newfound food lifestyle. At work I commit to my team and colleagues and give them my best while reminding myself that I come first in the event that should I overdo it.

This is my everyday being. Everyday being is waking up every day and deciding who I want to be. Some days I fail, and that's OK! And that's because at each failure, I learn more about myself, and by using the tools that I have learned, I become a better version of myself tomorrow.

I wrote this book to help others know that they are not alone in their struggles. It's OK to acknowledge that you need help to get you through the difficult times. Many of us hide our past in chapters to fit a certain mold and blend into society. However, doing that keeps us from being our best selves for ourselves and the people we love. Know that you are not alone. There is no shame in your past or present. Find your everyday being. Take care of your mental and physical health and, most importantly, ask for help and support.

As my story evolves, I move forward each day with a positive outlook. I have found my joy, yet my transformation will continue until my last days in this physical dimension, always learning new things about myself and others and putting into practice ideas and actions that add to my positivity. And I look forward to experiencing the finale!

ACKNOWLEDGMENTS

IN ALL MY BOOK IDEAS (and I've had several), I never thought I'd have an acknowledgment page. Acknowledgments always come off as cheesy and ungenuine—we get it; everyone matters. But that's why they are printed for all to see—because everyone does matter. The difficult part is this: How do you acknowledge the entire universe? So, with a little cheese and a lot of generosity, here are my acknowledgments:

To my favorite person and best friend, Mike Jones, who has always supported me without judgment and lets me "do me." Thank you for allowing me to appreciate the rainy days!

To our kids—Tino, Joey, Alex, Toni, and Lathan and Tyler—you each have your own stories to tell. You are so strong and smart. Thank you for your love.

To our grandchildren, Hayden and Braxton, you bring so much joy to my life!

To our dogs—Rex, Decker, Larry, and Scooter/Boogie—all rescues, who are rambunctious and chaotic at times; you've also found your groove in our pack.

To my parents and siblings—Francesco, Tindara, Rosetta, Gina, and Carmelo—I wouldn't be me without you, and I love you all very much. You built the foundation of my soul, and I'm thankful for every piece of yours that you gave for me.

An extra acknowledgment goes to my sister Rosetta for her seemingly never-ending positive energy. She is the kindest human being I have ever known, and her daughters have been blessed with those same qualities.

To my in-laws—Mary Lou, Mark, Melanie, and Allison—and to my husband's beautiful extended family. Thank you for welcoming me into your family. You are my home here in Colorado.

To all my girlfriends! While we don't see each other often, you have seen me at my best of times and at my worst of times. You are all woven together in my heart and in my life throughout these pages. I care for each of you very much, and I know you care about me the same. Dayna, a true friend and great listener whom I can always count on giving me a new perspective. Tina, whom I have relied on in so many ways and who is always there for me. Sharon, who introduced me to Mike, my beautiful husband. The girls at Bear Creek Village—all so unique, strong, and beautiful. You all stand out. Tricia, my best friend from back East and whom I think of often. My high school besties—Janet, Cathy, Carol, and Marci—and the rest of the girls. We had so many adventures, and I tell our stories often. My girls from upstate—Regetti, Willie, Beanie, Lenny, and Cas—we were friends the instant we met and had some crazy times on the vineyard. "V is for vacation!"

To my friends at Texaco, where I spent many long hours and after-work happy hours. We were a family, and you are all still in my heart. To all the friends I made on the road when I was traveling during my career at Hyperion—you know who you are—thanks for keeping me company on those long weeks away from my family. You made an impact on me, and I remember those times well.

To my editors and book team—Danielle Fetherson, KNLiterary, Karen Lacey, Bessie Gantt, Tom Locke and Polly Letofsky—who have encouraged me to go deep into my experiences and helped me get these words into writing and guided me through the world of publishing. The care you gave to every word and details throughout the process astounds me!

And to everyone else in the universe whom I have had encountered along the way: you all matter.

INSPIRATIONS

USUALLY AT THE END OF A BOOK there are pages for recommended reading. It's hard to say any one book or author has inspired me since so many things and people have inspired me. In my book, I'd like to share with you some of the things and people that exude positivity and inspire me, in no significant order:

Me

My husband, kids, grandkids, family, and dogs

My parents and siblings

My girlfriends

Dr. Mote and his team at Cornerstone Health Community

Star Trek

William Shatner

Oprah
Dr. Oz
Deepak Chopra
Louise Hay
Wayne Dyer
Don Miguel Ruiz
Steve Harvey
Ellen DeGeneres
John Lennon
Yoko Ono
George Foreman
Mike Dooley
Kyle Gray
The Dalai Lama
Piers Anthony
A good comedy
Rob Dyrdek
Macy Gray
Mary J. Blige
David Bowie
KRS-One
King Arthur
Merlin
Gandalf
Walking
Hiking
Geeky tech manuals/blogs
Discover magazines
Time
Alan Watts

Carlos Castaneda
Gavin Stephenson
Tut
Esther and Jerry Hicks
Meditation
Sunsets
The beach
Every song in this book and many more that I sing in my head at a moment's notice, inspiring me and keeping me focused on my goal of staying at peace.
So many other things
And trees—

If you've been inspired by this book, resonated with my story or experienced a mindful shift, I would love to hear from you. I've set up a page on our website where you can share what you've learned about yourself. Writing your thoughts for all to see can be challenging – but could you be encouraged knowing that you may touch someone else by doing so?

Take the Reader's Challenge today and help someone else not feel alone. https://www.myeverydaybeing.com/book/the-lotus-tattoo-readers-challenge.

Together, we are not alone.

INVITE MARISA TO
YOUR BOOK CLUB

As a special offer to *The Lotus Tattoo* readers,
Marisa has offered to visit your book club
whether online or in person.

Please contact Marisa directly to schedule
an appearance at your book club at
mjones@marisajones.co

ABOUT THE AUTHOR

MARISA JONES IS A SUCCESSFUL IT professional who leads global enterprise technology solutions for large organizations. Her passion includes driving transformational technology initiatives, writing and teaching workshops, and training and speaking engagements.

Born and raised in New York in an immigrant Sicilian family with an alcoholic parent, she faced many traumas that led to a turbulent life until she faced her victim mentality and replaced it with a new mind-set of positivity and balance. Marisa has started on a new mission of sharing the story of her life to inspire others and help them experience the same kind of healing she did.

Marisa has recently begun working with a local organization that provides domestic violence victims with the support they need to find healing in their lives and to rebuild their families. In her new partnership, she will work with the team to create workshops and programs for those coming out of abusive relationships. She also serves as a champion in her technology company's Diversity and Inclusion group, where she plans to use her personal story to support workplace initiatives to help individuals overcome personal challenges that can impair workplace success.

Marisa currently lives in Colorado with her husband, Mike, and their four dogs, and they enjoy spending time there with their four children and two grandchildren. To partner with Marisa or hire her to speak at your event, you can visit her online at marisajones.co.

EverydayBeing

Together, we are not alone

Everyday Being is a new platform offering content and resources to support those looking for inspiration and healing.

Our Mission

Our mission is to let people know they're not alone and show them ways to live without the fear or anger of their past trauma or abuse.

To build a community of resources for healing to victims of trauma to assist in their journey through teaching and forming human connections, inspiring them to embrace their beauty, and touch the lives of those around them.

Visit myeverydaybeing.com
And Join the Everyday Being Circle of Friends!

Ten years ago I made a commitment to heal and started on a journey to rid myself of the fear and anger I held onto for many years after the abuse. I was alone and had no idea how I was going to 'fix me', yet determined to try.

Today my life is transformed. My mind is at peace and I look at the world and those around me positively. Each day still carries its challenges. Balancing a family, raising kids, dealing with elderly parents and working full time can be stressful. None of those have changed, yet how I react to them has.

In my healing journey, I have found the tools and resources to help me maintain my peace and integrate these into my busy life.

What I hope to teach you is how to be in the moment, always. So you can feel the joy of a day in the park with your kids, or the pleasure of a night out with friends, in every moment of every day in your life.

What I hope to instill in all of you is an awareness of who you are deep inside your soul. The part of you that you can trust to keep your sanity in this chaotic world, and allow you to make decisions that support your needs, so you can better support those around you that need you.

My transformation will continue until the end of my life on this earth. We are all teachers and students. My learning never stops and I have so much to learn from each of you.

Join me on this journey, to find your everyday being, and in doing so you will be supporting me in mine.

Together, we are not alone.

Marisa